Art Inspired by Re

Hilary Ansell

Acknowledgements

I would like to thank the many children from Kingfisher Primary School, whose work has been photographed for this book. A big thank you also to the staff at Kingfisher for all their support and ideas.

I would like to thank the parents, children and staff of Edlington Family Centre for the loan of the Flower Hanging (page 60) and Copley Junior School for the loan of the School Pond (page 57).

Thank you also to my family for their great patience and support despite the mounting piles of rubbish!

Painted Glass Jars and Bottles (page 38)

Wire Jewellery (page 68)

Published by Collins, An imprint of HarperCollins*Publishers*
77 – 85 Fulham Palace Road, Hammersmith, London, W6 8JB

Browse the complete Collins catalogue at
www.collinseducation.com

© HarperCollins*Publishers* Limited 2011
Previously published in 2005 by Folens as 'Art of Recycling'
First published in 2000 by Belair Publications

10 9 8 7 6 5 4 3 2 1

ISBN-13 978-0-00-743944-7

Hilary Ansell asserts her moral rights to be identified as the author of this work

British Library Cataloguing in Publication Data
A Catalogue record for this publication is available from the British Library

Every effort has been made to trace copyright holders and to obtain their permission for the use of copyright material. The authors and publishers will gladly receive any information enabling them to rectify any error or omission in subsequent editions.

Editors: Elizabeth Miles/Nina Randall   Cover design: Mount Deluxe
Page Layout: Suzanne Ward   Photography: Kelvin Freeman
Line drawings: Sara Silcock (Linda Rogers Associates)

Printed and bound by Printing Express Limited, Hong Kong

Mixed Sources
Product group from well-managed forests and other controlled sources
www.fsc.org Cert no. SW-COC-001806
© 1996 Forest Stewardship Council

FSC

Contents

Introduction

Throughout the latter part of the twentieth century there was a growing awareness of the importance of conserving the world's natural resources for future generations. The 'throwaway' society of today is increasingly being urged to recycle everyday waste materials such as paper, card, rags, glass, tin, aluminium and plastics.

The *aim* of this book is to show how domestic waste materials can be reused and made into creative and very cost-effective artwork, attractive gifts and useful craft objects. The ideas are grouped into sections according to the main type of waste material used in the activity, although some activities will use more than one kind of waste.

The creative use of many of these waste materials can be directly related to folk art, history and the work of well known artists. For example, the mosaic activities, both paper and ceramic, can be related to Greek, Roman or Aztec cultures and also to the work of the architect and artist Anton Gaudi. The water lilies made from the bottoms of plastic drinks bottles would tie in beautifully with a study of Monet's paintings. The dried flower arrangements in glass jars were inspired by nineteenth-century exhibits in the local museum, as were the découpage activities.

The book offers activities for the individual, small groups, class activities and even whole school projects for special occasions such as anniversaries. The activities can also be modified to suit most age groups. There are also endless possibilities for varying the ideas.

A few weeks before the beginning of a project encourage the children to start collecting the relevant waste materials and sort them according to type. It is useful to sort fabrics, wools and plastic bags according to colour and store them in clear plastic containers for easy identification. Beads and buttons also look attractive stored in clear plastic jars.

It is hoped that whilst developing the ideas presented in this book, the children's imaginations will be stimulated and their skills extended. However, the most important aspect will be the opportunity for the children to be creative and have fun. I hope, too, that this book will inspire you to take a fresh look at your old rubbish!

Snakes and Caterpillars (page 50)

Handmade Paper

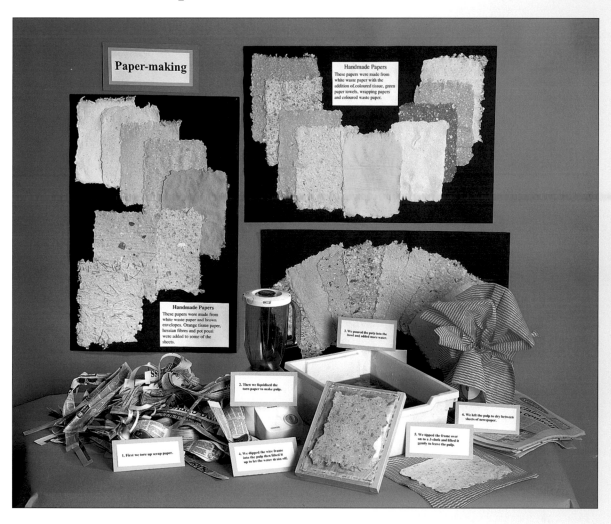

Approach

⚠ **An adult should operate the liquidiser.**

Resources
- Newspapers
- Liquidiser
- Large plastic container or storage box
- All-purpose cleaning cloths
- Paper-making frame (see page 6 for instructions on how to make your own frame)
- Sponge

1. Tear black-and-white newsprint into small pieces, place them in a liquidiser and fill the liquidiser with water. Liquidise for about 15 seconds until the pulp looks like grey porridge.

2. Pour the pulp into the plastic container and add a jug of water.

3. Repeat this process until you have enough pulp, remembering that the thicker the pulp the thicker the paper will be.

4. Spread a wad of newspaper on the table beside the container. Place an all-purpose cloth on top.

5. Keeping the paper-making frame horizontal with the mesh side uppermost, dip the frame into the pulp and pull it out again, draining off the excess water.

6. Tip the pulp onto half of the all-purpose cloth. Fold over the other end of the cloth to cover the pulp. Quickly sponge up any excess water.

7. Place a newspaper on top and repeat the process to build up a pile of handmade paper and newspaper. When the newspaper has soaked up the water from the sheets of pulp, the all-purpose cloths containing the pulp can be separated from the newspaper and spread out to dry. When dry, peel the sheets of handmade paper from the cloths.

Handmade Papers
These papers were made from white waste paper with the addition of coloured tissue, green paper towels, wrapping papers and coloured waste paper.

Variations

- Add coarsely liquidised coloured pages from comics or newspaper colour supplements to the grey pulp.
- Add torn up sweet wrappers, scraps of coloured tissue or waste display paper.
- Instead of black-and-white newsprint use coloured newspapers. Try mixing varying amounts of each.
- Empty the contents of a hole punch into the pulp.
- Add small fallen leaves, dried grasses or pot-pourri.
- Add short lengths of silk and sewing cottons.

Handmade Paper Using White Waste Paper

Gather together any white waste paper, for example the contents of a waste-paper basket, computer waste and discarded drawing and writing paper. Any writing, colouring or printing does not matter as it will add only a tinge of colour to the paper. Then proceed, using the same method as for Handmade Paper (page 5).

Variations

- To make fawn- or beige-coloured papers, add a used brown envelope at the liquidising stage.
- Leaves and grasses look particularly good mixed with the beige pulp.
- Add a small amount of liquidised coloured tissue to the white pulp.
- Save tea bags and add their contents to the white pulp. Experiment with the ratio of pulp to tea. Alternatively, dab dried sheets of paper with a wet tea bag to stain them brown.

Handmade Paper Mounts

Mount observational drawings of natural objects on handmade and brown wrapping papers.

Paper-Making Frames

To make your own paper-making frame cut four pieces of wood to the required size for the frame. Nail or screw the lengths together. Staple aluminium reinforcing mesh (as used in car repairs) to the frame. This should hold the frame rigid. Alternatively, use nylon ballet net but make sure the net is stretched very tightly as it will give when wet.

Mounted Treasures

All children love collecting things. A school visit, a walk in the park or a trip to the woods or seaside provide ample opportunities to collect a myriad of little treasures. Such found objects look most attractive when mounted on handmade paper and used to make unusual cards or pictures.

Resources
- Variety of beige speckled handmade paper
- Scraps of natural hessian (burlap)
- Brown wrapping paper
- White card
- Glue stick and PVA glue

Approach

1. Tear off a piece of handmade paper slightly smaller than the prepared white card.

2. Cut a piece of hessian smaller than this and fringe it around the edges. Glue the hessian to the handmade paper. Glue both of these onto the white card.

3. Glue the chosen object onto the hessian with PVA glue.

4. Experiment with different combinations of mounts.

Framed Treasures

Some of the larger found objects will look most attractive mounted in natural frames. Glue the white card on which your treasure has been mounted onto a piece of brown carton card. The brown card must be slightly larger than the white card. Cut or break some cane, dowel or twigs to fit around the card with overlapping ends. Glue the ends together and, if using twigs, wind string around the joins when the glue is dry. Glue the frame in position and tie string to the top of the frame for hanging.

Other Treasures

Not all treasures are natural found objects. They could be beads from a broken necklace, the buttons from a favourite garment, a scrap of fabric or lace, a badge or bottle top. They can be whatever the children treasure for whatever reason.

Button and Bead Cards

Resources
- Variety of handmade paper
- Buttons and beads (from broken necklaces)
- Cotton thread and needle
- White card
- Glue stick or PVA glue

Approach

1. Sew two or three buttons or several beads onto a piece of handmade paper.

2. Use a simple straight stitch to sew the stems and leaves of the flowers. Add smaller stitches between the stems for grass.

3. Glue the paper to the white card.

Recycled Greetings Cards

This is an excellent way of reusing favourite greetings cards.

Resources
- Variety of handmade papers
- Assortment of greetings cards
- White card
- Glue stick or PVA glue

Approach

1. Choose a simple motif and cut or tear it out carefully. To blend the edges of the motif into the handmade paper it is better to tear the motif from the greetings card.

2. Tear a piece of handmade paper slightly larger than the motif.

3. Use a glue stick to fix the motif centrally onto the paper.

4. Glue the paper to the card and trim to size if necessary.

Cast Paper Bowls

Resources
- Paper-making materials (see page 5)
- Small plastic bowl or basin
- Cling film

Approach

1. Make the paper pulp as described on page 5. Make sure the pulp is thick.

2. Cover an upturned bowl or basin with cling film to prevent the pulp from sticking to the bowl.

3. Spread a wad of newspaper on the table beside the container of pulp. On this place an all-purpose cloth.

4. Dip the frame into the pulp, lift out and drain the excess water. Tip the pulp onto the cloth. Lift off the frame.

5. Press the layer of pulp with the sponge to absorb as much water as possible.

6. Pick up the all-purpose cloth by two corners with the pulp still sticking to it. Flop it, pulp-side down, over the cling-film-covered bowl. Starting at one corner very carefully peel the cloth off the pulp. Gently pat the pulp around the shape of the bowl or leave it standing away from the bowl.

7. Leave the paper pulp bowl to air dry on the plastic bowl.

Decorating the Bowls

1. If the bowls are to be painted they need to be sealed. Once the paper bowl is absolutely dry brush the outside with a coat of PVA glue. When this is dry take the paper bowl off the plastic bowl and paint the inside with PVA.

2. Once sealed, the bowls could be painted with household white matt emulsion. This gives a good base for further painting.

Variations

- Mix PVA glue with powder or ready-mixed paint and paint the bowl with this.
- Torn or faded coloured papers from display boards can be used to make ready-coloured bowls that will need the minimum of decorating. These bowls need not be sealed.

Papier Mâché Balloon Vases

Resources

- Newspapers
- Newspaper colour supplements (glossy)
- Balloons
- Masking tape
- Cellulose adhesive
- Container on which to balance the balloon
- Petroleum jelly or washing-up liquid
- PVA glue or clear varnish

⚠ **Avoid wallpaper pastes as these often contain fungicides.**

Approach

1. With a marker pen draw a line around the narrow end of an inflated balloon to mark the neck of the vase.

2. Tear newspaper colour supplements into small pieces.

3. Smear the balloon with petroleum jelly or washing-up liquid to prevent the balloon from sticking to the finished vase. Next, paste the scraps of paper with cellulose adhesive (coloured side down) to the balloon.

4. Add two further layers of newspaper. If time allows it is best to leave the paste to dry between layers.

5. Now twist a sheet of newspaper into a rope and join with masking tape to make a ring large enough to fit around the base. If the vase is dry use masking tape to fix it in place, otherwise paste it in place with strips of newspaper.

6. Apply two more layers of newspaper, making sure that the base is well covered.

7. Add a final layer of colour supplement paper. Leave to dry thoroughly.

8. Burst and remove the balloon. Seal the vase with a coat of PVA glue or clear varnish.

Variations

- Use coloured tissue for the final layer.
- Use newspaper for the final layer, then paint with white emulsion. Decorate with painted patterns or pictures.
- To make handles: After stage 5 twist up another sheet of newspaper and tape it to the side of the vase when the vase is dry. Trim and tape the ends down. Continue with stages 6, 7 and 8.
- To make a jug: After stage 5 cut a triangle of thin card. Fold the triangle in half. Using masking tape secure the card to the vase, opposite the handle. Trim away the side of the vase inside the spout. Continue with stages 6, 7 and 8.
- To make a trophy shaped vase turn the balloon the other way up so the narrow end is the base.

Papier Mâché Elephants

Approach

1. Draw an elephant on thick card. Younger children will probably need a template. Cut it out.

2. Spread PVA glue on a small area of the elephant. Tear off pieces of newspaper and scrunch up fairly tightly. Press these onto the glued area. Repeat this process until the whole of the card is covered. If necessary add another layer so that the elephant is well padded.

3. Tear strips of newspaper and paste these over the screwed up paper using cellulose paste or diluted PVA. Take the ends of the paper strips over the edges of the elephant and paste to the reverse side of the card. Paste several layers of newspaper strips. Leave to dry thoroughly.

4. Paint with white matt emulsion as a base coat (optional). Paint as desired and decorate with scraps of fabrics such as velvets and silks. Stick on sequins, beads and braid.

Resources
- Thick card, for example grocery carton card
- PVA glue
- Newspapers
- Cellulose paste
- White matt emulsion
- Scraps of fabric, braid, sequins or beads

Variations

This method can be used to create any animal. Simply draw the shape and proceed as above. Use wool to add manes and tails or to create a fleecy coat, or add paper scales to make a reptile.

Paper Pulp

The pulped method of papier mâché is very good for modelling and sculpting and gives a coarser texture than the layered method.

Resources
- Newspapers (broadsheets are stronger than tabloids)
- Bucket for soaking the paper
- Sieve
- PVA glue
- Bowl and metal spoon (the newspaper ink will stain a wooden spoon)

Approach

1. Tear sheets of newspaper into small pieces, just cover with water and preferably leave to soak overnight, although this is not essential.

2. Squeeze and work the wet paper with your hands until it starts to disintegrate into a pulp.

3. Pour the pulp into a sieve and drain and squeeze out as much water as possible.

4. Put the squeezed-out pulp into a bowl and mix with PVA glue until the mixture binds together.

Note: Paper pulp activities are best done in small groups because of the large quantities of pulp needed.

Paper Pulp Masks

Approach

1. Draw a face shape onto an inflated balloon, making sure that the eyes are not too far apart.

2. Balance the balloon horizontally on top of a container and tape it down. The pulp is heavy so the balloon will topple over if not balanced correctly.

3. Smear the balloon with petroleum jelly to prevent the pulp from sticking to it.

4. Apply the pulp a little at a time starting around the eyes and along the nose area. Gradually work it out towards the sides of the face.

5. Add more pulp to build up the nose, forehead, cheeks and chin. Leave to dry for at least a week.

6. Paint and decorate as desired.

Resources
- Paper pulp
- Round balloon
- Petroleum jelly
- Container on which to balance the balloon
- Masking tape
- Felt-tipped pens

Paper Pulp Beads

Resources
- Paper pulp
- Narrow plastic drinking straws or cotton buds
- Petroleum jelly
- White matt emulsion
- PVA glue or clear varnish

Approach

1. Smear petroleum jelly around a straw; if using cotton buds snip off the bud and then smear the stick.

2. Using a little of the pulp, form a bead-shape around the straw. You will be able to shape several around one straw. Try making round, oval and cylindrical beads of different sizes. Leave to dry for a week.

3. Paint the beads with white emulsion while still on the straw. This gives a good base for further painting.

4. Paint in bright colours as desired. Leave to dry.

5. Coat with PVA glue or clear varnish. Several coats of clear varnish give a good finish.

6. Ease the beads off the straw and thread to make necklaces and bracelets.

Paper Pulp Wall Plaques

Approach

Resources
- Paper pulp
- Newspapers
- Plate
- Petroleum jelly
- White matt emulsion
- PVA glue or clear varnish

1. Smear a plate with petroleum jelly. Tear some strips of newspaper, dip them in water and cover the plate. This will stop the pulp from sticking to the plate.

2. Press the pulp evenly onto the plate to the depth of about a centimetre. Add a loop of string at the top of the plate, burying the ends well in the pulp. A relief pattern can be built up at this stage or the pulp can be left smooth. Leave to dry in a warm place for about five days.

3. Ease the paper pulp from the plate. Use diluted PVA glue to apply a top layer of small pieces of newspaper. Leave to dry.

4. Apply one or two coats of white matt emulsion as a base for painting. When dry, paint on a pattern or picture. When the plate is thoroughly dry varnish well.

Paper People

Resources
- Newspapers
- Thin knitting needle or long-handled paintbrush
- Masking tape
- Cellulose paste
- White matt emulsion

Approach

1. Using a long-handled paintbrush or knitting needle to get started, tightly roll a double sheet of newspaper and twist into a 'rope'. Fold it up until you have a sausage shape about 20 centimetres long. Secure the ends with masking tape.

2. Squeeze the sausage shape about a quarter of the way down and bind with tape to create a neck.

3. To make the arms and legs, roll up and twist further 'ropes' of paper. Cut to the required size and tape them to the trunk. Bend up the ends to make the feet.

4. Cover the figure with strips of pasted newspaper. Pad the head with screwed up pieces of paper held down with strips. Wind longer strips around the arms and legs. Leave the figure to dry for a few days.

5. Coat with white matt emulsion to give a good base for painting. When dry, draw the neckline, cuffs and waistline of the clothes. Paint as desired.

Paper Animals

Approach

1. Roll up a double sheet of newspaper and twist it into a 'rope'. Fold it up into a flat sausage shape, leaving one end of the 'rope' sticking out for a neck. Secure with masking tape. If the neck piece is long enough, curl the end under and tape it to form the head, otherwise tape a piece of screwed-up paper onto the end of the neck piece.

2. For the legs of the animal, twist up another sheet of paper, cut to the required size and tape in place over the body piece. Make sure that the animal will stand up. Trim as necessary.

3. Paste layers of paper around the form to give a fuller shape and smoother outline. Leave to air dry.

4. Paint with white matt emulsion to give a good base for further painting.

Resources
- Newspapers
- Thin knitting needle or long-handled paintbrush
- Masking tape
- Cellulose paste
- White matt emulsion

Textured Trees

If possible, take the children out to look closely at and feel the textures of tree bark. If this is not possible, show them photographs and illustrations of trees and highly textured barks. Generate a discussion as to how these textures might be recreated on paper.

Resources

- Strong paper or thin card
- Paints
- Newspapers
- PVA glue
- Wood shavings (optional)
- Coloured paper, tissue, magazine pages
- Sawdust or sand (optional)

Approach

1. Roughly sketch the tree on a strong paper or card background. Colour-wash the background of the picture and leave to dry.

2. Twist sheets of newspaper into 'ropes'. Glue several of these side by side to create the tree trunk. Spread out the top ends to create the branches and spread the bottom ends slightly for the base.

3. Tear up small scraps of newspaper. Screw up and glue these around the base of the tree to represent rough grass. Wood shavings could be used instead.

4. Mix appropriate colours and paint the tree and grass, taking care to stipple the paint into all the folds of the paper.

5. The trees can be left bare for a winter scene or seasonal foliage can be added by gluing on scraps of coloured paper, tissue or magazine pages as leaves or blossom.

6. A textured foreground can be created by mixing sawdust or sand with paint and a little PVA glue.

Exploring Tone and Colour

Newsprint Town

Resources
- Newspapers
- Glue stick
- Black paper
- Black felt-tipped pen

Approach

1. Discuss the kinds of buildings found in a town, talking about features such as size, shape and windows.

2. Draw a townscape using clear bold shapes, or draw individual buildings and assemble them into a townscape.

3. Select different shades of grey print from the newspapers. Cut these into small squares and use them to fill in the shapes of the buildings.

4. When complete, cut around the outline of the town. Mount on black paper for a dramatic effect.

5. If necessary, use a fine, black felt-tipped pen to define the windows, doors or edges of buildings.

Complete This Picture

Resources
- Newspaper, magazines or travel brochures
- White drawing paper
- Glue stick
- Soft leaded sketching or colouring pencils

Approach

1. Cut out a photograph from a newspaper, magazine or travel brochure. (You may wish to have these cut out before the lesson begins.)

2. Fold this in half and cut.

3. Using a glue stick, glue half the picture onto white drawing paper.

4. Using a ruler complete the outline of the photograph on the paper.

5. Complete the picture using the sketching or colouring pencils. Try to match up the shades of grey or colour so that it is difficult to tell where the original picture stops and the drawing begins.

Exploring Colour with Magazines

This idea combines mathematics and artwork. Children can explore tessellating shapes, such as squares, equilateral triangles and hexagons, while working with shades of a particular colour or within a particular range of the colour wheel, for example dark green through to yellow.

If studying the body, they could be asked to search for different hair colours or to fill a sheet with eyes or faces.

Resources
- Card (cartons/cereal boxes)
- Catalogues, magazines, wallpaper oddments
- Glue stick

Approach

1. Create a template by cutting the desired tessellating shape out of the centre of a piece of card. Use the hole in the card as a window through which to view the motifs you want to cut out.

2. Use the window or template to draw as many shapes as you require.

3. Cut out the shapes and glue them onto paper to make a tessellating pattern.

Celebrity Portraits

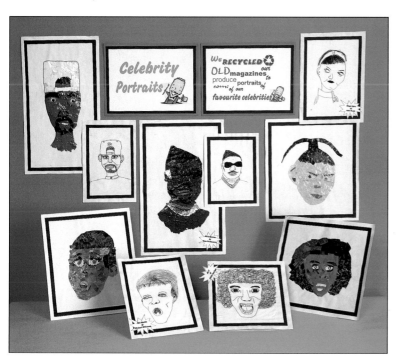

Approach

1. Carefully study the picture of a chosen celebrity and make a pen drawing, noting which areas need to be shaded.

2. Now using a pencil make a large but simple line drawing of the celebrity to be covered with magazine pieces.

3. Tear out a variety of flesh tones from magazines and cut them into small squares.

4. Glue the squares onto the pencil drawing, overlapping the squares to make sure that no white paper shows. Follow the curves of the drawing.

5. Seal the whole picture with a coat of PVA glue.

Resources
- Colour magazines
- White paper
- Handwriting pens
- Glue stick, PVA glue

Découpage Containers

The popular nineteenth-century craft of découpage provides an ideal way of recycling paper, such as old magazines, shopping and seed catalogues, and oddments of wallpaper and wrapping paper. Plastic and card containers can be transformed into pencil or paintbrush cases and boxes for storing treasured items.

Resources
- Magazines, catalogues, wallpaper, wrapping paper
- Tall, cardboard cylindrical container with lid or cardboard box with lid
- PVA glue or clear varnish
- Ribbon or braid

Approach

1. Cut out images of a specific type, such as cars, flowers, toys, clothes or sports personalities.

2. Using an old bristle paintbrush and slightly diluted PVA glue, start to cover the container with the images. Work on a small area at a time. The cut-outs can be wrapped over the top edge of the container but need to be trimmed to fit along the bottom edge. Make sure that none of the original container shows.

3. Finish by painting all the découpage area with PVA glue or clear varnish.

4. Trim with ribbon or braid.

Découpage Desk Tidy

Resources
- Cylindrical card tubes or plastic containers of different sizes
- Large round card, metal or plastic lid in which to sit the above
- Collection of cut-out magazine images
- PVA glue or clear varnish

Approach

1. Stand several cylindrical containers in the large lid. You might need three, four or five containers, depending on their sizes. Try out various arrangements.

2. Cover all the components of the tidy with the cut-out magazine images.

3. Group the containers and glue them together. Leave to dry.

4. Apply glue to the base of the containers and to the inside edge of the lid where the containers touch it. Glue the containers in position. When dry, coat with PVA glue or clear varnish.

Découpage Baubles

Resources
- Newspapers
- Magazines, catalogues
- Cellulose paste
- Ribbon or synthetic raffia
- PVA glue or clear varnish

Approach

1. Scrunch a double sheet of newspaper into a ball and squeeze tightly. Tear several hand-sized pieces of newspaper and paste them around the ball, squeezing well each time. Try to keep the ball as solid as possible. Using a pencil, make a small hole in the top of the ball in which to glue the hanging thread.

2. Cut out pictures of flowers or other images from magazines and catalogues. Snip around the edges of the pictures so that the cut-outs will fit smoothly around the ball.

3. Paste the cut-outs around the ball, taking care to overlap them so that no newspaper shows.

4. Cut a length of ribbon or raffia for the hanger. Fill the hole at the top of the bauble with PVA glue and poke the raffia or ribbon hanger into place. Tie a bow of ribbon or raffia. Glue on the bow to cover the hole.

5. When completely dry, paint with PVA glue or clear varnish to give a glazed surface.

Découpage Frames

Resources
- Thin card
- Cut-out images from magazines, catalogues or wallpaper
- PVA glue

Approach

1. Complete an observational study in pencil, paint or coloured pencil.

2. Cut a rectangular piece of thin card. It should be large enough to form a border around the original drawing.

3. Paste the paper cut-out images around the outside of the card to the desired width. When dry, carefully cut around the inside edge of the frame. Trim the outside edges straight or cut around the pasted images.

4. Cut a piece of backing paper or card to the same size as the frame. Mount the picture on this and add the frame.

Magazine Spill Boxes

Approach

1. With the least colourful side of the paper facing you, roll a page of magazine paper around a knitting needle or paintbrush handle (start at one corner and roll to the opposite diagonal corner). As you proceed, use the glue stick along the edges of the paper and along the diagonal. Always roll the paper around the knitting needle a couple of times before adding any glue otherwise the spill will not slip off the needle. Hold the paper firmly around the needle as you are rolling it so that the spill does not become too slack. When rolled and glued, slip the spill from the needle. Make several spills in this way.

2. Measure the depth of the container and cut the spills into shorter lengths to fit the sides. It is a good idea to do this with the lid on as you will probably need to leave a clear space at the top of the container for the lid to fit.

3. Spread PVA glue onto one section of the container at a time and arrange the spills vertically, making sure that they touch each other and none of the underlying container is showing.

4. Now cover the lid with spills. In the case of margarine containers or ice cream tubs which have a ridge around the lid, just cover the central depression.

5. In order to hide the cut edges of the spills glue braid or lace around the top and bottom of the boxes and around the lid.

Resources
- Coloured pages from glossy magazines or colour supplements
- Lidded container such as margarine or ice cream tub
- Thin knitting needle or long-handled paintbrush
- Glue stick
- PVA glue
- Oddments of braid or lace

Spill Beads

Resources
- Coloured magazine pages
- Thin knitting needle or long-handled paintbrush
- Glue stick
- Sewing needle
- Strong, coloured thread

Approach

1. Cut the coloured magazine pages into long, thin triangles and narrow strips.

2. Roll a strip of paper around a knitting needle or paintbrush handle, starting at the base of the triangle. Make sure the brightest side of the paper is showing on the outside of the roll. Run the glue stick along the centre of the strip as you roll. The number of beads required to make a necklace will vary according to the size of the bead but 20 beads is a good amount to start with.

3. Thread the beads onto strong thread. To add variety, sew through the ends of some beads so that they will hang down. The beads can be threaded in rows to make collars or threaded onto elastic to make bracelets.

Paper Spills Frame

Approach

1. Cut a piece of carton card larger than the mirror.

2. Glue the mirror to the card with latex glue. Alternatively, use double-sided adhesive tape.

3. Roll up coloured magazine pages into paper spills (see Spill Boxes, page 20).

4. Cut the spills to size and use PVA glue to stick them around the mirror.

5. Trim the outside edges of the frame with braid.

Resources
- Carton card
- Old vanity mirror
- Latex glue
- Double-sided adhesive tape
- PVA glue
- Coloured magazine pages
- Oddments of braid

Magazine Mosaics

Resources
- Stiff paper or thin card
- Magazines, catalogues, travel brochures
- Glue stick

Approach

1. Draw a simple design on the paper.

2. Select the required coloured pages from the magazines and cut into small squares no bigger than 1 centimetre square.

3. Following any curves in the design, position and glue the squares leaving small gaps in between.

4. Fill in the background areas by gluing the mosaic pieces down in straight rows.

Mythical Mosaic Monsters

Draw a mythical creature on black sugar paper. Keep the design simple. Select pages from magazines and wallpaper sample books and cut into small squares. Following the curves of the design, fill in the creature with the coloured squares.

Mosaic Masks

Approach

Resources
- Round balloon
- Petroleum jelly
- Newspapers
- Cellulose paste
- Black sugar paper
- Magazines
- PVA glue

1. Draw a face on an inflated balloon and smear the balloon with petroleum jelly.

2. Dip newspaper pieces in cellulose paste and place them on the balloon. Add two layers, leaving the eyes and mouth free.

3. Twist up some newspaper to make a nose shape and paste it on with strips of newspaper. Similarly, build up the forehead, cheek bones and chin.

4. Add three more layers of newsprint. Then add a final layer of black sugar paper. Leave to dry thoroughly.

5. Burst the balloon and remove the mask.

6. Select coloured magazine pages and cut into small squares.

7. Thinly cover a small area of the mask with PVA glue and start applying the squares.

8. Complete by filling the eye and mouth holes with tissue paper or leave them open if the mask is to be worn.

Wallpaper Townscapes and Wax Rubbings

Resources
- Variety of textured wallpapers
- PVA glue
- Wax crayons

Approach

Townscapes

1. Draw buildings and townscapes on textured wallpaper and cut out. Encourage the children to consider the wide variety of shapes that are found in a town.

2. Assemble the buildings onto background paper, shuffling them around until a satisfactory arrangement is found. A discussion about perspective might be useful here.

3. Glue down carefully on black paper and leave to dry.

Wax Rubbings

1. Position a large sheet of white paper over the wallpaper picture. Tape to the desk with masking tape. This prevents multiple images as the paper moves.

2. Rub lightly with a coloured wax crayon, for example red or brown. Keep the crayoning parallel to the edge of the paper. Repeat this process using a black crayon, rubbing a little more heavily on the edges of the buildings for definition.

3. Remove the rubbing from the wallpaper picture and apply a very watery colour wash. This has to be very delicate otherwise the rubbing will be obliterated.

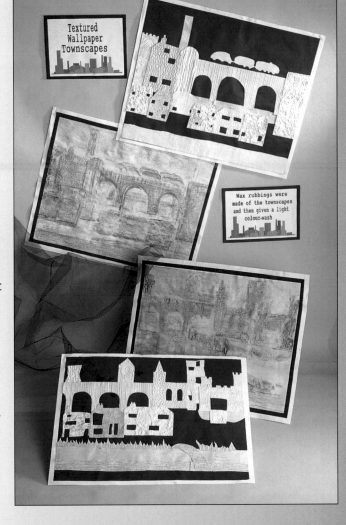

Wallpaper Reptiles

The method used for making the wallpaper townscapes (see above) can be adapted to suit many topics. Anaglypta wallpaper with a pebbly or scaly pattern is ideal for reptiles, dragons and dinosaurs.

Approach

1. Cut out a large reptile from highly textured wallpaper.

2. Place this underneath a sheet of white paper and rub over with wax crayons. The reptile can be reversed to create a creature going in the opposite direction. The rubbing pattern will also be different. Smaller reptiles can be cut out and rubbed to create a group of creatures.

3. Rubbings can be mounted as they are or a background can be drawn in with wax crayons and then the whole picture colour-washed.

Printing on Wallpaper

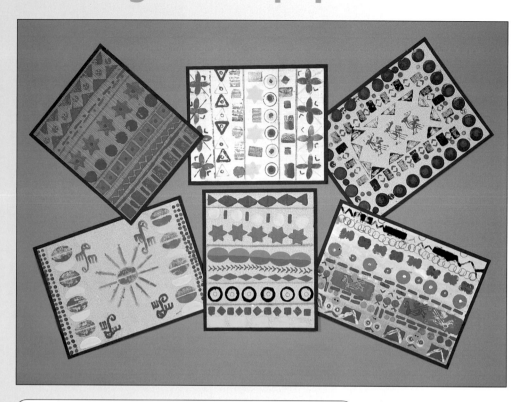

Lightly textured wallpaper provides an interesting surface on which to print as it imitates the texture of fabric. Unprinted or very light wallpapers will need a colour-wash but brightly coloured papers can be printed on very successfully provided that strong, contrasting colours are used. These designs were inspired by Aztec and Mexican cultures.

Resources
- Collection of items that can be used as printing 'blocks', for example: bottle tops, dowelling, small wooden blocks, scraps of wooden beading, bits of sponge
- Printing inks, ready-mixed paint or thickly mixed powder paint with PVA glue added

Approach

1. Colour-wash the wallpaper if necessary. Leave to dry.

2. Apply paint to the printing block by dipping it in paint or applying the paint to the block with a brush. Print in rows or around the edge of the paper.

String Printing Blocks

Resources
- Oddments of string or cord
- Offcuts of wood or strong cardboard cartons
- PVA glue

Approach

1. Design a simple motif to fit the block of wood or carton card.

2. If using card, cut two or three pieces to the same size and glue them together to create a block which is easy to hold.

3. Draw the motif onto the wood or card. Glue the string over the design. Leave to dry thoroughly. Check for any loose ends.

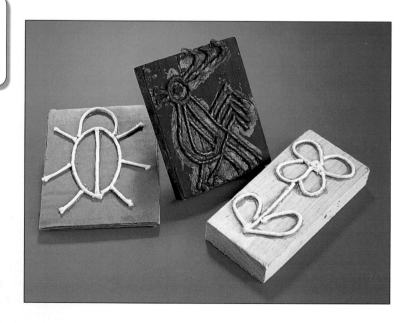

Food Tray Windows

Resources

- Polystyrene food tray
- Scenes from magazines (optional)
- Clear adhesive tape, PVA glue
- Thin card
- Scraps of fabric, braid or fringing

Approach

1. Cut the bottom out of a polystyrene food tray.

2. Draw or paint a view the same size as the bottom of the tray or cut a scene from a magazine. Glue this to thin card.

3. Tape the card into the polystyrene frame.

4. From the discarded base cut narrow strips of polystyrene and glue these onto the view to form the struts of the window frame.

5. Cut narrow strips of fabric to fit each side of the window. Sew along the top edges, gather and either sew or glue in place. Glue a scrap of braid or fringe across the top edge of the tray for a pelmet. Add curtain tie backs if desired.

Display Trays

This is a novel way of displaying collections of small objects.

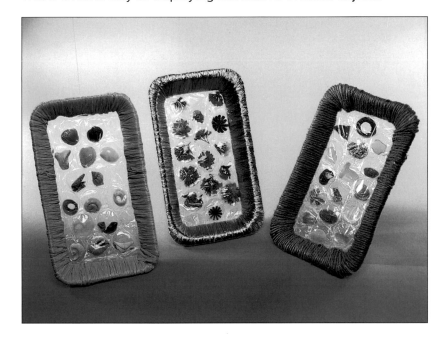

Resources

- Polystyrene food tray
- String, yarn or synthetic raffia
- Large bubble wrap
- Clear adhesive tape, PVA glue

Approach

1. Cut the bottom out of a polystyrene food tray.

2. Wrap the remaining frame using string, raffia or yarn.

3. Cut a piece of large bubble wrap to fit the frame.

4. Make a slit at the back of each bubble and insert the items to be displayed. These could be shells, pebbles, dried flower heads, seeds or even small toys. Secure the slits with clear adhesive tape.

5. Tape the bubble wrap into the frame.

Polystyrene Press Prints

This is an effective way of making use of polystyrene packaging that comes with household appliances. The packaging will have to be cut into handy-sized blocks. Polystyrene food trays can also be used.

Indian inspired
polystyrene
press prints

Approach

Resources
- Polystyrene blocks or food trays
- Water-based printing ink
- Print rollers and trays

1. Decide upon a motif and using a ballpoint pen or blunt pencil slowly press the design into the polystyrene. Make sure that it is well indented and that the lines are sufficiently wide so that they will not clog with ink.

2. Squeeze some ink onto the tray and roller well. You should be able to hear the ink pull back from the roller. Roll the ink across the polystyrene block.

3. To print, place the block ink-side down onto the paper and press gently. Carefully lift the block off the paper. Roll more ink onto the block and place it face down, edge to edge with the first print. Continue in this way until the paper is filled.

Weaving with Plastic Bags

Place Mats

Approach

Resources
- Carton card
- Oddments of brightly coloured wool
- Brightly coloured plastic bags

1. Cut the card to the required size allowing an extra 2 centimetres on the width and length.

2. Mark the top and bottom edges of the card at 1–centimetre intervals. Cut slits in the card at these marks to the depth of 1 centimetre.

3. Attach brightly coloured wool to the card loom by winding several times around the first 'tooth'. Bring the wool to the front of the card through the first slit. Take it down to the bottom of the card, through the first slit, behind the 'tooth' and out through the second slit. Now take the wool up to the top of the card and into the second slit, behind the 'tooth' and out through the third slit. Continue in this way until the loom is warped. Finish by winding the wool several times around the last 'tooth'.

4. Cut the plastic bags into strips 5–6 centimetres wide and weave under and over the warp threads leaving the ends of the strips sticking out at the sides. Push the strips down well after every few rows.

5. When the card is full, secure the ends of the strips by tying them together in bunches of three or four with brightly coloured wool.

6. Slip the weaving off the card loom by bending the 'teeth' forwards and slipping the wool from behind.

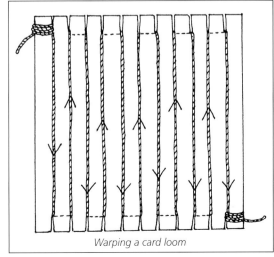

Warping a card loom

Lidded Boxes

These boxes are constructed from rigid plastic mesh used in gardens. As the mesh is 1 centimetre square the box nets can be easily worked out on 1-centimetre-squared graph paper.

Resources
- Graph paper
- Plastic mesh
- Brightly coloured plastic bags

Approach

1. Draw the box net on graph paper. Cut out each side separately.

2. Cut the pieces of box from the plastic mesh.

3. Loosely lace the sides of the box to the base using wide strips of plastic carrier bag. Bring the sides up and lace together. Lace the lid to the top of the box.

4. Using wide strips of plastic bag weave in and out of the box until all the holes are filled.

Plastic Baskets

Resources
- Plastic ice cream or margarine container
- Brightly coloured plastic bags
- Felt or fabric
- PVA glue

Approach

1. Cut down the sides of the container to the base at about 2-centimetre intervals, thus creating stakes on which to weave. Make sure you have an odd number of stakes.

2. Cut two differently coloured carrier bags into strips about 5 centimetres wide.

3. Slip one of the plastic strips behind a stake and out through the two slits. Leave the shorter end (about 6 centimetres) to the left. Slip a strip of the second coloured bag behind the next stake to the right and repeat so that you have a short end and a long end of plastic appearing through the same slit. Now take the long end of the first colour across the stake to the right, behind the next stake and out to the front again. Repeat this with the second colour. Repeat this process until the basket is woven. The strips have a tendency to ride up, so push them back down periodically. To join new strips, merely slip the new length behind the last stake used, leaving the short ends at the front to be darned in afterwards.

4. To complete the basket, cut a circle of felt or other brightly coloured fabric and glue this into the bottom of the container.

Hanging Baskets

These can be made using the plastic baskets described on page 28 or by simply painting ice cream or margarine containers.

Resources
- Plastic ice cream or margarine containers
- Plastic bags
- Chicken wire
- String or yarn
- Clear adhesive tape, PVA glue

Approach

1. Paint the plastic container using paint mixed with PVA glue. Leave to dry.

2. Using a bradawl, pierce three equidistant holes under the rim of the container. Tie on lengths of string and knot together to form the hanger.

3. Crumple up a small piece of chicken wire to fit into the tub. Using different shades of green plastic bag, cut wide strips and cut into fringes. Roll or gather these up to look like plants or tufts of grass. Secure the bottoms with tape or staples. Push the tufts into the holes in the chicken wire.

4. Make smaller versions of the plastic bag carnations described below and push these into the chicken wire. Hang the baskets from the ceiling.

Variation
A simpler version of these can be made using a strip of thin card about 10 centimetres wide, instead of the plastic container. Decorate the card by painting or covering with wallpaper. Tape tufts of greenery and flowers along the top edge of the strip. Join the ends of the card together with double-sided adhesive tape or glue. Leave as a plant pot or tie on yarn to hang.

Plastic Bag Flowers

Approach

1. Cut a plastic bag into strips about 6–7 centimetres wide (wider if the plastic is thin) and 22 centimetres long. One carrier bag makes a large flower.

2. Gather the strips into a bunch. Hold them halfway along and twist the end of the stem wire tightly around the plastic strips, thus holding them all together.

3. Bend both ends of the bunch of strips upwards and hold together by twisting tightly around with thin wire or adhesive tape.

4. Wind florists' tape or strips of crêpe paper around the base of the flower and along the stem.

5. Trim the flower to shape.

Resources
- Coloured plastic bags
- Adhesive tape or thin wire for winding
- Thicker wire for the flower stems
- Florists' tape or crêpe paper

Plastic Pom-Poms

Approach

1. Draw two concentric circles on thin card. The centre circle needs to have a diameter of at least 2 centimetres. Cut around the outer circle, then cut out the inner circle. You will need two of these discs to make a pom-pom.

2. Cut plastic bags into strips about 3–4 centimetres wide.

3. Holding the two discs together, start to wind the strips through the centre and around the card. Continue winding in different colours until the hole is filled up.

4. Now cut through the plastic around the edges of the discs. Pull the discs slightly apart. Tie a length of yarn firmly around the loops between the discs and secure with a knot. Finally, pull the discs away and trim the pom-poms if necessary.

Cheer Leader Pom-Poms

1. Cut plastic bags into strips about 2–3 centimetres wide. Cut the bag across its width, cutting through the front and the back at the same time to make lots of circular strips. Cut these once to open them out.

2. Gather together about 20 strips and tape them halfway along their length. Fold them in half at the point where they have been taped. You will need at least four of these bunches to make a pom-pom.

3. Tape the folded strips around a dowel or broom handle. Make sure they are secure. If a cardboard tube is to be used as a handle, tape the folded section of the strips into the opening of the tube. Tape extra bunches of strips around the outside edge of the tube.

4. Finish by winding strips of brightly coloured fabric around the handle. Glue at the ends.

Resources
- Brightly coloured plastic bags
- Clear adhesive tape, PVA glue
- Short lengths of thick dowel, broom handle or sturdy kitchen roll tubes
- Brightly coloured fabric

Plastic Jewellery

Resources
- Clear plastic tubing
- Coloured plastic bags
- Clear adhesive tape, PVA glue
- Plastic drinks bottles
- Coloured sequins

Plastic Tubing Necklaces and Bracelets

Approach

1. Cut a length of clear plastic tubing long enough to go over the head or round the wrist.

2. Use a pencil or knitting needle to push twisted scraps of coloured plastic bag into the tube. Start by filling up the middle, working from both ends. Secure the last piece of plastic bag at each end with PVA glue.

3. Hold the ends of the tubing together and tape with clear adhesive tape.

Variation

Cut the tubing into short lengths to make individual beads. Dab a spot of PVA glue onto each twist of plastic bag before squeezing it into the tube. When the glue is dry, thread the beads onto brightly coloured thread.

Plastic Drinks Bottle Bangles

Approach

1. Cut 4–5-centimetre-wide rings off a plastic drinks bottle.

2. Wind strips of plastic carrier bag around them until well padded. Tape the end.

3. For a striped effect wind another coloured strip at an angle over the first colour. Glue on sequins for further decoration.

Plaited Necklaces and Friendship Bracelets

Approach

1. Use thin, flimsy plastic bags as they plait very easily. Cut the bags into strips and plait three colours together. Try experimenting with strips of different widths.

2. Join the ends and tape together with clear adhesive tape.

Fire and Water Hangings

Resources
- Ring or metal coat-hanger on which to hang the fabrics and plastics
- Assorted materials such as bubble wrap; clear, opaque and white plastic bags; nets, chiffons and silks; and interesting yarns

Approach

1. If using a coat-hanger pull it into a round shape. Bind the ring or hanger with wool or narrow strips of fabric.

2. Tie three or four lengths of yarn to the ring to suspend it.

3. Cut long, narrow strips of assorted materials. Fold the strips in half and attach to the ring by passing the two ends through the loop and pulling tight (see diagram).

4. Thread shiny beads onto some of the strips. Thread large sequins onto invisible thread. Continue until the ring is full. Create the fire hanging in the same way, using red, orange and gold materials.

Jellyfish

Resources
- Wire
- Clear and coloured plastic bags
- Yarn
- Clear adhesive tape
- Nylon thread

Approach

1. Bend a length of wire and tape the ends together to make a ring.

2. Make the skirt of the jellyfish as described in Fire and Water Hangings, incorporating pink, purple and blue shades of plastic.

3. To make the body, stuff a clear plastic bag with opaque plastic bags and a few strands of pink and blue yarn. Pull into shape and knot securely. Use clear adhesive tape to fasten the body to the ring.

4. Thread a nylon line through the top of the body and hang.

Waterfall Hanging

Resources

- Coloured fabrics
- Blue hessian background
- Toy filler or chopped tights
- Embroidery thread
- Latex glue
- Yarn
- Materials for stick weaving (page 43) and bobbin knitting (page 46)
- Green plastic bags
- Bubble wrap
- Clear, opaque and white plastic bags
- Nets and other matching materials

Stones

Cut out irregular shapes from 'stone' coloured fabrics. Sew around the edges, leaving a gap for stuffing. Turn right side out. Stuff with toy filler or chopped tights. Sew up the opening. Stitch the stones with green embroidery threads to represent moss. Fix to the background with latex glue.

Water and Sky

Work these areas in a variety of long and short stitches using different shades and textures of knitting yarn. By working on a blue background fabric, not all the areas have to be stitched.

Trees

Make strips of stick weaving and bobbin knitting to the required length (see pages 43 and 46). Lay on the background and twine and twist to create a suitable shaped trunk. Glue into position with latex glue.

Foliage

Cut green plastic bags into strips about 6 x 10 centimetres and, working from the back of the hanging, poke the ends of the strips through to the front (see Pegged Squares, page 52). When you have finished pegging, clip the leaves to the desired length.

Waterfall

Cut long narrow strips of bubble wrap, clear, opaque and white plastic bags, nets and other matching materials. Start near the bottom of the waterfall and working across its width sew these materials on in short lengths. Gradually work up the waterfall, increasing the length of the strips. Some materials, such as smooth plastic bag or net, will thread through a large-eyed needle and can be sewn directly into the background fabric. Others, such as bubble wrap, will need to be folded in half and tacked on at the fold.

Plastic Bottle People

Resources

- Newspaper
- Plastic bottles of various sizes
- Flesh-coloured nylon tights and fabric
- Oddments of fabric, lace, fringing, braid, wool and beads
- Sand
- Card
- PVA glue

Approach

1. Screw up a sheet of newspaper into a tight ball. Cut a leg off a pair of tights. Push the ball into the toe. Twist the ball around several times and pull the leg of the tights back over the ball. Repeat until you cannot see the newsprint through the tights.

2. Trim off any excess fabric and glue or stitch the ends down.

3. Partly fill a plastic bottle with sand to make it stable.

4. Push the head into the second leg of the tights. Twist and pull through as before. Place the head on top of the bottle, pulling the tights down over the bottle to the base.

5. Twist the tights at the side of the bottle near the bottom and pull back over the bottle and over the head. Repeat this process until the leg has been used up. Finish at the base and stitch or glue the ends underneath. Bind with tape or thread around the neck to keep the head in place.

6. Cut a length of fabric long enough to gather around the bottle for the dress. Trim with lace or braid as required. Gather the fabric around the neck and tie tightly.

7. Cut a length of card for the arms. Cut out hands from the card and cover with flesh-coloured fabric. Glue these to the arms. Cover the arms with fabric and glue or sew to the back of the doll. Bend the arms around and attach them to the sides of the doll.

8. Add wool for hair, felt pieces for features and jewellery if desired.

Plastic Bottle Fish

Resources

- Thin plastic drinks bottles
- White paper
- Fine permanent felt-tipped pens
- Masking tape
- PVA glue
- Curtain ring
- Thin white paper or tissue
- White paper reinforcement rings
- Coloured drawing pins
- Nylon fishing line
- Ready-mixed paint or powder paint

Approach

1. Cut away the base of a plastic bottle. Flatten the bottle from the cut edge to the shoulder, making sure that the creases are squeezed out as flat as possible.

2. To make a pattern for cutting out the fish, lay the partly flattened bottle on a sheet of white paper and draw around it. The tail and fins of the fish can now be drawn to fit within this outline. Cut out the fish-shaped pattern.

3. Place the pattern on the flattened bottle and draw around it onto the bottle with a permanent marker. Hold the edges of the bottle tightly together and cut away the unwanted pieces. Still holding the cut edges together, secure with overlapping strips of masking tape.

4. Attach the curtain ring to the top of the fish with masking tape. The children will need to experiment to find the point of balance.

5. Use diluted PVA glue to cover the fish with small pieces of thin white paper or tissue paper. Put a stick or long-handled paintbrush into the mouth of the fish, prop it up in a jar and leave to dry.

6. When the fish is dry apply a base coat of ready-mixed or powder paint mixed with a little PVA glue. Two coats may be needed to cover the bottle thoroughly. When this is dry paint on spots, stripes or other patterns. Use white paper reinforcement rings or coloured drawing pins to create the eyes. Thread nylon fishing line through the ring and hang.

Variations

Larger fins can be cut out of card and foil scales can be added. Use buttons, beads and glitter for further decoration. Feathery tails can be made from strands of tissue paper, plastic bags or wool.

Plastic Bottle Vases

Approach

1. Cut the neck and shoulders off a plastic bottle.

2. Tear colour supplement pages into smaller pieces and glue them, colour side down, to the bottle. Make sure they overlap the cut rim of the bottle. When the bottle is covered add two layers of newsprint. Let this dry before adding a final layer of colour supplement paper. Allow to dry thoroughly.

3. Mix some paint to match the colour of the bottle's covering. Use a dry sponge to dab the paint sparingly over the bottle, blending all the colours together.

4. When thoroughly dry, coat with clear varnish or PVA glue making sure that it is well sealed on the inside rim. Apply a second coat when dry. The vase should now be watertight and ready for fresh flowers.

Lilies or Bottle Neck Flowers

Resources
- Plastic bottles
- Pipe-cleaners
- PVA glue
- Green paper
- Flexible straws
- Green garden sticks or thin dowel
- Clear adhesive tape
- Acrylic paint or emulsion paint
- Green florists' tape

Approach

1. Cut the neck and shoulder off a bottle. Snip the lower edge into spiky petal shapes.

2. Bend the ends of three pipe-cleaners to form stamens. Glue and roll the other ends of these in a strip of green paper to form a plug for the neck of the bottle. Push into position.

3. Tape the flexible end of the straw to the back of the flower shape so that it stands out from the flower. Use small strips of tape and build up the back of the flower slightly. Bend the straw so that the flower head hangs down.

4. Slip the straw over a garden stick.

5. Paint the flowers using acrylic paint or household emulsion. Paint the tape at the back of the flower green and paint the straw or bind it with green florists' tape.

Plastic Bottle Flowers

Resources
- Plastic drinks bottles with fluted bottoms
- Flexible straws
- Green garden sticks or thin dowel
- Clear adhesive tape
- Acrylic paint or emulsion paint
- Green florists' tape

Approach

1. Cut the bottoms off the bottles and shape them to resemble petals.

2. Continue to make the stems as described for Lilies or Bottle Neck Flowers (page 36).

3. Slip the straw over a garden stick. If the stick is too thick, slit the straw to ease the stick in. Secure with tape.

4. Paint the flowers using acrylic paint or household emulsion. Paint the tape at the back of the flower green and paint the straw or bind it with green florists' tape.

Variation

Choose bell-shaped yoghurt pots and snip v-shaped pieces out of the rim. Proceed as above.

Monet's Water Lilies

Resources
- Plastic bottles with fluted bottoms of various sizes
- Acrylic or vinyl paint
- PVA glue
- Green paper or card
- Clear plastic packaging (optional)

Approach

1. Cut the bottoms off various sizes of bottles and shape into flowers. Three different sizes work very effectively together.

2. Using acrylic or vinyl paint colour the sections of the flower. When dry, use PVA to glue the three sections inside each other.

3. If you want to float the flowers on water cut the leaves from clear plastic packaging and paint with vinyl paint, otherwise use green paper or card.

37

Painted Plastic Containers

Resources
- Clear, rigid, plastic containers
- Water-based glass paints and outliner paste
- Fine brushes
- White paper
- Adhesive putty

Approach

1. Cut pieces of paper the same size as the faces of the box to be painted. If the container is cylindrical simply measure its circumference and cut paper to fit. Draw the design on the paper and fix to the inside of the container with adhesive putty.

2. Using the outliner paste, follow the lines of the design. Leave to dry.

3. Colour in the design with glass paints.

Painted Glass Jars and Bottles

These make attractive storage jars or nightlight holders. Bottles may be painted and used as candleholders. (See also Acknowledgements, page 2.)

 Never leave children unsupervised with burning candles.

Sand Jars

Resources
- Glass jar
- Sand
- Powder paint
- Acrylic paint
- PVA glue

Approach

1. Colour the sand by simply mixing with powder paint. Mix up a dessertspoonful of powder paint with several tablespoonfuls of sand.

2. Fill a jar with the layers of coloured sand using a funnel.

3. Tilt the jar to create slopes and different levels. Move the jar gently to avoid mixing the layers of sand.

4. Fill the jar right up to the top so there is no space between the sand and the lid. If any space is left the sand will move when the jar is handled.

5. Using a fine brush and acrylic paint or powder paint mixed with PVA glue; paint a picture on the jar to complement the layers of sand.

6. Decorate the lid of the jar with coloured card or felt.

Snowstorms

Resources
- Small screw-topped jar
- Plastic modelling clay
- Latex (waterproof) adhesive
- Glitter
- Felt

Approach

1. Decide upon a scene and model the pieces out of plastic modelling clay. Dry as instructed on the packet.

2. Draw round the lid of the jar onto a piece of felt. Cut out the circle of felt and glue it to the outside of the lid.

3. Coat the inside of the lid with waterproof adhesive and arrange the models to create a scene. Leave to dry.

4. Fill the jar about three-quarters full with water (do not fill the jar completely as the model will displace some of the water). Sprinkle in some glitter and mix well. Top up with water so that the jar is almost full.

5. Coat the outside rim of the jar with adhesive and screw the lid on tightly. Leave to dry overnight.

Decorated Glass Jars

Tissue-Covered Jars

Resources
- Glass jars
- Coloured tissue paper
- PVA glue or cellulose paste
- Black marker pens
- Clear varnish (optional)

Approach

1. Cut coloured tissue paper into small straight-sided shapes. Use either dilute PVA glue or cellulose paste to glue them to the jar.

2. When the jar is dry use a black marker pen to outline the shapes.

3. Coat with PVA glue or clear varnish.

Foil-Covered Jars

Resources
- Glass jars
- Thin card
- Kitchen foil
- Double-sided adhesive tape
- PVA glue
- Shoe polish or paint

Approach

1. Cut a motif out of thin card and attach it to a jar with double-sided tape.

2. Cut a piece of foil to fit all the way around the jar. Crumple the foil lightly and then very carefully straighten it out.

3. Spread glue across the motif and around that section of the jar. Press the foil onto the motif and rub gently, working the foil well in around the edges of the card.

4. Glue the foil all the way around the jar.

5. Cut out a motif for the lid and cover this in the same way.

6. Rub the motifs with a little shoe polish on the tip of a finger or use a dab of paint.

Sequinned Jars

Resources
- Glass jars
- Assortment of sequins and seed beads
- Glitter
- PVA glue
- Shiny card or paper

Approach

1. Coat the jar with a thin layer of PVA glue and cover with sequins, seed beads and glitter.

2. To decorate the lid cut strips of shiny card or paper and use PVA glue to glue them around the sides of the lid.

Victorian Dome Jars

Victorian Dome Jars are an attractive way of reusing large screw-topped jars. They are best made when there is a plentiful supply of dried grasses and seed-heads to be found in gardens and hedgerows. However, with a little forward planning, flowers such as statice, helichrysums and poppies can be grown in the school garden or in containers, and cut and dried for use later in the year.

Resources
- Large screw-topped jar
- Assortment of dried flowers and grasses
- Oasis
- PVA glue
- Adhesive tape
- Oddments of braid or fringing

Approach

1. Cut a piece of oasis to fit in the lid of the jar. Glue this in position with PVA glue.

2. Cut the flowers to an appropriate length, remembering to measure them against the jar. Start in the centre of the oasis with the tallest flower and work around. The jar will probably be viewed from all sides. Cover as much oasis as possible. Helichrysums can be nipped off their stalks and pins pushed through the heads to anchor them. Occasionally place the jar over the arrangement to make sure that it is not getting too wide.

3. When the arrangement is complete screw the jar into the lid. Seal with adhesive tape. Glue fringing around the jar to hide the lid.

Peg Loom Weaving

Weaving is just one of the ways of using up an accumulation of odd scraps of wool. These brightly coloured weavings were inspired by the textiles of Mexico and were worked on a peg loom.

Resources
- Peg loom
- Strong yarn or smooth parcel string
- Oddments of brightly coloured wool

Approach

1. To warp up the loom, use strong yarn or smooth parcel string. For each warp, measure off a length of yarn twice the length of the finished weaving plus 10 centimetres at each end for the fringe or finishing off. For example, for a finished weaving 30 centimetres in length cut a length of yarn 80 centimetres in length for each peg (60 cm plus 10 cm for each end). Thread each peg with the length of yarn, knotting the two ends together (see diagram a). Place the pegs in the holes in the base. Bring all the warp threads to the front.

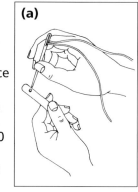

(a)

2. To weave, wind in and out of the pegs from one side to the other (diagram b). When the pegs are nearly full lift the first peg out of the base and pull the warp thread up through the weaving until it is visible at the top of the weaving (diagram c). Put the peg back in the hole (diagram d). Repeat with each peg. The weaving will now be on the warp threads at the front of the loom. Continue and repeat the process until the warp threads are full.

3. To finish off, remove all the pegs and lay the weaving flat. Gently pull the warp threads through the weaving until there is enough thread at each end to fasten off. Make sure that the weaving is smoothed out and even. Knot the protruding warp threads in threes or fours.

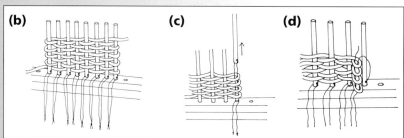

(b)   **(c)**   **(d)**

Stick Weaving

Resources
- Peg loom sticks, or thin sticks such as wooden dowel and adhesive tape
- Yarn
- Oddments of brightly coloured wool

Approach

1. If peg loom sticks are available use three or four sticks. Thread the sticks in the same way as for the peg loom (see page 42). If you do not have peg loom sticks improvise by taping single strands of yarn to the bottoms of thin sticks such as wooden dowel. Use the tape sparingly.

2. To weave, hold the sticks about halfway up and fan them out slightly. Hold the end of the weft thread in the same hand until you have got started. Weave in and out of the sticks, working from one side to the other.

3. When they are full, draw the warp thread up through the weaving. Continue in this way until the warp threads are full. Finish as for peg loom weaving. If making a belt sew the ends in for a neat finish and attach a buckle.

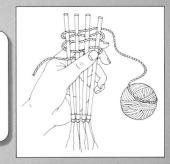

Drinking Straw People

This is a variation on the Stick Weaving idea above.

Resources
- Six long chenille pipe-cleaners
- Four fat plastic drinking straws
- Scraps of felt and oddments of wool
- Tapestry needle

Approach

1. Thread a pipe-cleaner through each of the four straws, making sure that they stick out at each end. At one end the pipe-cleaners need to stick out enough to form the legs.

2. Twist all the pipe-cleaners together at the other end, where the head will be. Push the straws up to this end. Spread the straws out in a fan shape but not too widely.

3. Thread the needle with wool suitable for hair or a hat and begin to weave under and over the straws at the head end. Change colour for the face and the clothes.

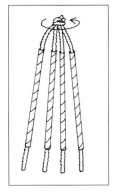

4. Do not weave right to the bottom end of the straw as you will need to grip the end to pull the straw off the pipe-cleaner. Slide the straws off the pipe-cleaners leaving the weaving in place. Twist the pipe-cleaners together in pairs to form the legs. Wrap the ends with wool to form the feet. Bend up.

5. To make the arms push a pipe-cleaner through each side of the figure. Fold each pipe-cleaner in half and twist. Turn the ends over for hands. Draw on the eyes, nose and mouth with felt-tipped pen or glue on tiny scraps of felt.

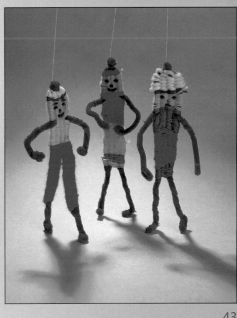

Weaving on Rings

Resources
- Suitable ring (hoop, bike wheel, lampshade ring)
- Masking tape
- Oddments of coloured wool

Approach

1. Wind wool all the way round the ring and knot or glue the end.

2. Warp up the ring to resemble the spokes of a wheel. The threads do not have to cross each other in the centre. It can be more effective if they cross off-centre. You will need to create an odd number of warp threads. To do this, instead of taking the last thread all the way across the circle, fasten it to where all the 'spokes' cross.

3. Start weaving at the centre of the ring where all the threads cross. Work around this bunch of threads until the centre of the weaving is quite firm. Weave out from the centre, working on two, three or five threads at a time. Leave gaps in the weaving.

4. Wind wool around some of the warp threads. Incorporate a wide variety of yarns and experiment using several yarns together. Stitch or tie on long threads and let them dangle. Create fringes and add beads.

Tree Rings

Resources
- Suitably sized ring
- Oddments of wool and a needle

Approach

1. Wind sky-coloured wool around the ring, covering about half the circumference. Knot or glue the end. Wind the bottom half with green or brown wool.

2. To create the warp threads, tie a length of wool to the ring where the sky and land colours meet. Keeping the wool taut, take it across the circle to the other side; wind it two or three times around the ring and return. Repeat until the area of land is warped.

3. To weave, turn the hoop so that the warp threads are vertical. Weave under and over them with land colours until the area is complete.

4. Turn the ring so that the land is at the bottom. Add the warp threads for the tree in a fan shape, stitching through the weaving and around the ring at the bottom and fanning out at the top. You will need about 12 warp threads. When weaving the trunk pull the warp threads in to keep the sides of the trunk fairly parallel. Create thicker or thinner branches by weaving along four, three or two threads.

5. Foliage or blossom can be knitted by casting on a lot of stitches and knitting three or four rows. Break off the wool leaving a long end. Pass the end back through all the stitches and draw up the knitting. Sew the gathered knitting to the tree. Another method is to use finger knitting (see page 56).

Hole-in-Card Looms

Resources
- Assortment of coloured wool
- Needle and thread
- Strong carton card
- Coloured hessian or woven cloth
- Felt fabric
- PVA glue
- Shells, beads, twigs, etc.

Approach

1. Cut a circle out of strong card.

2. Glue hessian across the card covering the hole. Cut out the middle section leaving enough fabric to turn to the back. Snip all the way round to ease the fabric. Turn it to the back and glue.

3. Working from top to bottom across the hole, create the warp threads by stitching into the hessian at the edge of the circle. Space the threads about 1 centimetre apart.

4. Weave a landscape scene and add detail to the scene by cutting out and gluing on fabric shapes.

5. Add detail in the foreground by stitching items such as shells and beads into the hessian.

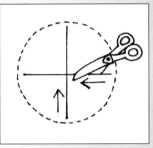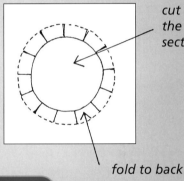

cut out the middle section

fold to back

Approach

1. Cut out a circle from card. Cut slits around the edge of the card at regular intervals, about 1 centimetre in length, making sure there are an odd number.

2. Bring the warping thread to the front of the card through one of the slits. Cross the circle to the opposite slit. Go into this, behind the 'tooth' and out through the next slit. Cross the circle again through the centre and into the next slit. Repeat this process until the circle is warped.

3. To create an odd number of threads do not take the last thread all the way across the circle but stop at the centre where the threads cross. Stitch or tie the end of the thread in here.

4. Start weaving around the point where all the threads cross and work out in a spiral.

5. When the card is full to the base of the slits knot a fringe to the edge of the weaving. This hides the carton card. Leave the weaving on the card to display.

Hot and Cold Planets

Resources
- Carton card
- Assortment of hot and cold coloured wool

French Knitting

To Make a Bobbin

Resources
- Short length of strong cardboard tube
- 4-cm long rust-resistant nails
- Masking tape, coloured plastic tape

Approach

1. Using a separate piece of masking tape for each nail, tape four, six or eight nails around the rim of the tube depending on the size of the tube. Make sure that at least 2 centimetres of nail is taped to the side of the tube. Push the tape tight against the nail.

2. Wrap a length of tape all the way around at the top of the tube. Wind coloured tape around the whole tube.

To Knit

Resources
- Bobbin
- Coloured wool and needle

Approach

1. To cast on drop the end of the wool down the tube and hold with the little finger of the hand that is holding the tube. Put the wool to the right of the nearest nail (left if left-handed), loop the wool around the nail and take it to the next nail right (or left). Loop the wool around this nail. Repeat this process until you are back to the beginning.

2. Hold the wool across the first nail, maintaining tension by using the index finger of the left hand to hold the wool to the side of the bobbin. Using finger nails or a blunt needle lift the bottom loop over the wool.

3. Turn the bobbin clockwise if right-handed (anticlockwise if left-handed), continually lifting the lower loop up over the wool. Hold the little tail of wool firmly with the little finger. Tug on it to pull the knitting through the tube.

4. To finish, break off the ball of wool. Thread the remaining length of wool onto a needle, pick up all the stitches from the nails and pull the wool through and fasten off.

Lengths of French knitting can be stuffed to make snakes and caterpillars. They can be used to make trees and branches. Long creepers can be made by sewing on felt leaves or leaves made from wire and old tights.

Pom-Pom Mice

Resources
- Thin card (cereal packets)
- Assortment of white, grey and brown wool
- Coloured felt
- Latex glue
- Needle and thread

Approach

1. Cut out two circles, 6 centimetres in diameter, from thin card. Make these into rings by cutting out central circles 2 centimetres in diameter.

2. Hold the two card rings together and wind wool evenly all the way round, passing it through the central hole each time.

3. When the central hole is full cut through the threads around the edges of the card rings.

4. Pull the card rings slightly apart. Tie a length of wool firmly around the wool between the card rings and knot securely. Tear the card away.

5. Cut out two head pieces from felt and sew around the curved sides. Stuff firmly. Using latex glue, stick the head to the pom-pom, pressing it well into the cut threads.

6. Cut out two ears, fold and either glue or stitch them to the head. Glue on the eyes. Twist strands of wool together for a tail and glue into position.

Hedgehog Family

Follow the same procedure as for the mice but make a 10-centimetre pom-pom for the mother hedgehog and a 6-centimetre pom-pom for each baby. Use several strands of beige and brown wool together when winding the pom-pom. Use brown felt for the face.

Wrapped Landscapes

Create landscapes around card. Portrait-shaped card will give depth to the scene.

Resources
- Thick carton card
- Double-sided adhesive tape
- Wool in landscape colours
- Felt scraps
- Glue

Approach

1. Stick a strip of double-sided tape down the middle of each side of the card.

2. Starting from the bottom wind wool around the card, pressing it to the tape. Use interesting textures as well as a range of shades. Wrap two shades of a colour together. Alter the angle of wrapping to create hills.

3. When the card is covered, cut out shapes from scraps of felt and glue them to the scene.

Stitched Cards

Resources
- Old greetings cards, postcards or magazine pictures glued to thin card
- Glue stick
- Embroidery cotton, thin needles

Approach

1. Using a straight stitch sew into the picture, embroidering the most important parts. Use larger stitches in the foreground and smaller stitches in the distance. Younger children will be happier using large images from magazines. They can then use thicker needles and yarn.

2. The finished pictures can be mounted in clip frames and given as presents or can be remounted on card to make greetings cards.

Fabric Collage Landscapes

Resources
- Thin card on which to glue the fabric
- Wide variety of natural coloured fabrics in interesting textures, for example corduroy, towelling and velvet
- Wool, braids
- PVA glue

Approach

1. Begin by gluing a strip of sky-coloured fabric at the top of the card.

2. Work down from the sky in layers, adding distant hills and fields in cool colours. Work brighter colours into the foreground. Make sure that the whole card is covered.

3. Add detail such as fences, trees, animals and buildings. Clip short pieces of green wool and glue along the bottom edge of the picture or along river banks and road sides.

Fabric Collage Portraits

Resources
- Thin card
- White paper the same size as the card
- Small patterned wallpaper
- Variety of fabrics, wool and beads
- PVA glue

Approach

1. Cut a piece of patterned wallpaper the same size as the card and glue it on.

2. On the white paper draw the head and shoulders of a celebrity. Draw in the features and the clothes. This is going to be used as a paper pattern.

3. Cut out the head and neck. Pin this to some flesh-coloured fabric and cut out. Glue this to the card.

4. Piece by piece, cut up the drawing and use as a paper pattern to assemble the portrait. Add wool for hair and beads for earrings and jewellery.

Flowers from Tights

These flowers can be made from coloured tights, or flesh-coloured tights can be treated with a pre-dye and then dyed the required colour.

Resources
- Coloured tights
- Thick and thin flexible wire
- Green wool or thread
- Pipe-cleaners
- Felt-tipped pens

Approach

1. Make a petal shape out of thin flexible wire. Twist the ends together.

2. Cut a piece of tights fabric twice as long as the petal and wider. Stretch the fabric over the wire and hold all the edges together at the bottom of the petal. Wind and tie tightly with strong thread or wool. Trim off any excess fabric. Make enough petals for a flower.

3. Cut some pipe-cleaners to make stamens. Cut a length of thick wire for the stem. Using green wool, bind the stamens to a petal and bind each petal to the stem. Continue winding the wool around the ends of the petals until all the tights fabric is covered and the back of the flower is built up. Wind along the stem and finish by tying the wool to the stem wire.

4. Flowers made from light-coloured tights can be drawn on with felt-tipped pens.

5. Leaves can be made in the same way as the petals and added to the stem.

Snakes and Caterpillars

These colourful creatures are simply stuffed tights decorated with scraps of felt.

Resources
- Coloured tights
- Toy filler or chopped tights
- Scraps of felt
- Glue
- Needle and thread

Approach

1. Cut both legs off a pair of tights. Pull one leg onto your arm then pull the other leg over the top. Remove the tights from your arm and give them a good stretch.

2. Stuff with toy filler or chopped tights and stitch up the end. For the caterpillar tie the 'sausage' into segments.

3. Add a forked tongue for the snake and glue on felt eyes and pattern detail to the body. Decorate with scraps of felt, tufts of wool, buttons and sequins.

Stuffed Faces

Resources
- Old tights
- Toy filler or chopped-up tights
- Buttons, wool, sewing thread and needle

Approach

1. Cut a leg off a pair of tights and stuff the toe end with toy filler to make a head shape. Twist the head around several times and pull the remaining length of tights back over the head. This makes a double layer of tights fabric. Fold the remaining end to the back and stitch down.

2. Either sew on buttons for eyes or cut them out of felt. To make the nose, pinch up a fold of fabric and stuffing and stitch through from side to side. Cut the mouth out of felt or stitch with red or pink wool. Add ears by stitching on little pads of stuffed tights. Stitch through the pads to create the folds in the ear.

3. Sew on strands of wool for hair. Add beads for earrings or bows in the hair. Make hats or add spectacles. The faces can be mounted on sticks for puppets or grouped together to make a class portrait!

Coat-Hanger Faces

Resources
- Wire coat-hanger
- Old tights in flesh tones
- Fur fabric or wool
- Felt
- Glue

Approach

1. Pull the wire coat-hanger into a face shape with the handle at the bottom. Bend the hook in to make a holding loop.

2. Cut a leg off a pair of tights. Put the loop into the toe and pull the tights up over the wire. Twist the head around several times and pull the tights back down over the head. Tie at the chin.

3. Stitch or glue features onto the head. Scraps of fur, fabric or wool can be used for the hair. Eyes and mouth can be cut out of felt and glued on.

Pegged Squares

Approach

1. Zigzag the edges of the hessian on a sewing machine, or bind with masking tape to prevent fraying.

2. To make the prodding tool, break one of the legs off a dolly peg. Sand the other leg to a tapering point.

3. Using a felt-tipped pen, draw a margin the width of a ruler all the way around the hessian square.

4. Cut the fabric to be pegged into pieces about 3 centimetres wide and 10 centimetres long.

5. Make a fold in the hessian just below the pen line. Crease it well and keep the fold uppermost. Poke the peg through both layers of hessian just below the fold to make a hole. Now poke one end of the short strip of fabric through the hole. Pull it halfway through. Check that it is of equal length each side of the fold. Repeat all the way along the fold to the pen line. Do not work in the margins. (See diagram above.)

6. Hold the fabric each side of the fold and pull so that the fold opens and the strips of cloth lie each side. At this point they look like bows but they will stand up as you work each successive row. Make another fold just below the first row and start again. Repeat until the square is complete. If desired, the pile can be neatened by clipping.

Pegged Squares Rug

When all the squares are completed they can be mounted individually, turned into cushions or joined together to make a class wall hanging or rug.

Resources
- 30-centimetre square pieces of hessian
- Dolly pegs
- Sandpaper
- Felt-tipped pens
- Large supply of material scraps

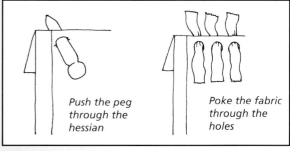

Push the peg through the hessian

Poke the fabric through the holes

Class Rug

Resources
- Frame
- Hessian
- Felt-tipped pens
- Masking tape
- Drawing pins
- Dolly pegs
- Sandpaper
- Large supply of scraps of material

1. Mark the design on a large piece of hessian using felt-tipped pens. Zigzag the edges or bind with masking tape to prevent fraying.

2. Attach the hessian to a frame with drawing pins, stretching it well. Balance the frame between two tables so that the children can sit with their knees under the frame. The pieces of fabric should be cut the same size as for Pegged Squares (page 52) but the method varies slightly.

3. Using a modified dolly peg (see page 52), poke a hole in the hessian. Take a short strip of fabric and use the peg to poke one end of the strip through the hole. With the other hand under the frame pull the strip halfway through. Now make another hole very close to the first and poke the other end of the strip through. With the hand under the frame pull both ends even. All that should be seen on the top of the hessian is a small stitch. The two ends are hanging down below. Now poke the peg into the last hole that was made and poke another strip of cloth into this hole. You now have two pieces of fabric in the same hole. Make a new hole next to this one and poke the other end of the strip through. Continue in this manner until the rug is completed.

4. Take the rug off the frame. Turn the hems to the back and either glue with latex adhesive or sew.

To Make a Frame

Frames are very easily made. They are simply four lengths of wood held together with bolts and wing nuts. Decide upon the dimension of the rug. Cut the wood to size, drill holes and bolt the lengths of wood together. A metre in length is quite ample and 60 centimetres is sufficient for the width.

Rainbow Squares

This is an opportunity to explore both colour and texture. It is ideal for a large group activity with each child contributing an individual piece to the final hanging.

Let each child choose the colour in which he or she wants to work. Ask them to start collecting things in shades of their own colour, such as beads, buttons, buckles, oddments of wool, coloured plastic bags, threads, parcel bows, florists' ribbon and artificial flowers.

Resources
- Children's collections (examples listed above)
- Carton card for looms
- Hessian
- Rug canvas
- Plain materials in various colours to use as a base on which to sew buttons, beads, etc.
- Embroidery needles, tapestry or large-eyed needles to take wool, weaving needles
- Latex glue
- Ready-mixed paint or powder paint

Canvas Squares

Paint a 16-centimetre square of rug canvas on one side with ready-mixed or powder paint in your chosen colour. Leave to dry. Using a wide variety of threads and materials stitch up and down through all the holes in the canvas. Vary the size, direction and type of stitch, (for example, running stitch, cross stitch and half cross stitch). Vary the texture by sewing with narrow strips of fabric, strips of plastic bag and different thicknesses of wool. Try using several strands of various shades together. Create further texture with the addition of buttons and beads.

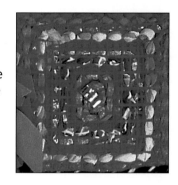

Button and Bead Squares

Create an interestingly textured square by sewing on numerous buttons, beads and sequins of various sizes. Cover buttons with material by cutting a circle a little larger than the button. Sew around this in running stitch until you are back at the beginning. Pull the thread so that the circle draws up into a little bag. Slip in the button. Pull up the thread firmly and stitch. Soft padded bobbles can also be made in this way.

Woven Squares

Cut an 18-centimetre square piece of carton card and make the loom as described for Place Mats (page 27). Keeping to shades of one colour, weave the square using wool, strips of fabric, plastic bags, florists' ribbon and so on. Do not leave the ends sticking out at the edges of the work. When the end of a row has been reached, weave back in the opposite direction, taking care not to pull against the end warp thread. When the end of a strip has been reached join a new one by overlapping the old for several centimetres and complete the row. Push the weaving down periodically to keep it firm. When the card is full, slip the weaving off by bending the 'teeth' forwards.

Fabric Collage

Make a collection of interestingly textured fabrics. Combine smooth, shiny surfaces of satin and taffeta with velvets and fur fabrics. A few small scraps of glittery fabrics would add highlights to the finished hanging. Small pieces of fabric may be sewn down randomly or a design may be developed using geometric shapes. Embellish with buttons, beads or even parcel bows.

Pegged Squares

Cut a hessian square 20 centimetres in size. Draw a 2-centimetre margin all the way around. Do not work in the margin. Neaten the edges to prevent fraying. Proceed as described for Pegged Squares (page 52), but work in shades of one colour. Combine plastic bags and fabrics. If desired, neaten the finished squares by clipping.

Assembling the Wall Hanging

An old dust sheet will make an excellent backing on which to glue the squares. Mark out the required area in 15-centimetre squares. This allows for the overlapping of squares so that none of the backing materials shows. Sort out the squares into colours and begin to lay them on the backing, working diagonally across the area. When satisfied with the arrangement stick down with latex adhesive as this remains flexible when dry.

The School Pond – A Textile Picture

This can be a whole school project with the children working on the picture a group at a time. Much of the picture can be worked separately and assembled later.

Approach

1. Draw and photograph a pond scene, perhaps in the school environmental area.

2. Cut a piece of hessian the size of the finished hanging plus an allowance for turnings and a slot at the top for hanging. Neaten the edges to prevent fraying.

3. Using felt-tipped pens, draw the design on the back of the hessian, remembering that it will appear reversed on the front.

4. Mark in the areas to be pegged, such as the rough grass, bush and area between the pond and path. Use drawing pins to attach the hessian to the frame.

5. Use the following methods for each area of the design.

Background Bushes and Foliage

Make lengths of finger knitting for bushes and foliage. To finger knit tie a loop in the end of the wool several centimetres from the end. Put the loop on the index finger. Hold the short end of wool just below the knot with the thumb and second finger. With the other hand pass the long length of wool over the index finger towards the front. Hold this with the finger and thumb whilst passing the first loop over the second (see diagram). Pull on the long end to reduce the size of the stitch. Thicker strands can be made by finger knitting the lengths of finger knitting.

Grass and Leaves

Using a variety of green fabrics, peg the grassy areas as described on page 52. Peg the leaves of the bush with green plastic carrier bags. Cut double leaf shapes from the bag and peg as for the grass.

Finger Knitting

Stone Wall

Cut stone shapes from grey fabric. Sew around the shape leaving a small opening for stuffing. Stuff the stone and sew up the opening. (See Waterfall Hanging, page 33.)

Trees

Using shades of brown wool make strips of French knitting (see page 46) and ordinary knitting sewn into tubes for the trunks of trees. Alternatively, strips of weaving can be made on weaving sticks (See Stick Weaving, page 43).

Pond

Cut a piece of fabric the size of the pond. Cut scraps of fabrics in blues, browns and greens and sew these to the pond background, or glue on for a quicker result.

Logs

Cut the logs out of textured brown fabric and stitch into them to add more texture.

Assembling the Parts

1. When the pegging is finished spread latex glue on the back of these areas to prevent pieces working loose. Leave to dry. Take the picture off the frame and turn it right side up.

2. Clip the grassy area by the pond very short.

3. Cut paving stones out of fabric and glue into position leaving small gaps between. Sew into these gaps with stone-coloured wool.

4. Glue the pond and the stone wall into position.

5. Twist up lengths of French knitting, stick weaving and knitting into a tree. Glue into position.

6. Cut a piece of plain green fabric such as velvet to the right size for the field. Glue into position. Only glue lightly around the edges because this will be stitched into.

7. Cut more double leaf shapes for the foliage of the tree. Poke these through the hessian from the back.

8. Using several shades of blue knitting wool, embroider the sky in a long surface stitch. (See Waterfall Hanging, page 33.)

9. Stitch on the finger knitting to form bushes on the skyline and behind the plastic bag bush. Glue or stitch on lengths of French knitting for the fence. Glue on the logs.

10. Cover any hessian that is showing with layers of stitching in wool of various shades of green. Stitch into the pond and give the impression of reeds.

11. When the picture is complete, turn back the hems and make a slot for a pole for hanging.

Textile Flowers – A Group Wall Hanging

The following textile work was inspired by a study of Van Gogh's *Sunflowers*.

Resources

- Assortment of fabrics
- Hessian
- Brown buttons and beads
- Brown thread, needle
- Toy filler or wadding
- Latex glue

Approach

1. Choose a fabric for the centre of the flower. Cut out a circle 8 to 10 centimetres in diameter.

2. Stitch the circle centrally to a 25-centimetre-square piece of hessian. Stitch on buttons and beads to cover the circle.

3. Cut strips of yellow material about 4 centimetres wide by 12 centimetres long. Fold in half and trim the ends to a petal shape. Working from the back, poke the petals through the hessian (for the method see Class Rug, page 53). Some children could work one row, others two, in order to create different flowers. A row of green strips may be worked around some of the flowers.

4. Cut around the flower heads leaving a 4-centimetre border of hessian. Snip this at intervals. Fold over and glue to the back of the flower.

5. Cut out the vase shape and sew to the background leaving the top edge of the vase open. Stuff the vase lightly with toy filler. Sew down the opening.

6. Glue the flower heads in position with latex glue.

Individual Wall Hanging

Resources
- Rectangle of blue hessian
- Assortment of fabrics
- Buttons and beads
- Thread in various colours
- Toy filler or wadding
- Latex glue
- Cane or pole for hanging

Approach

1. Pin and sew a rectangle of blue hessian, making a slot at the top to accommodate a pole or cane.

2. Sew the sunflower centre directly onto the blue hessian. Embellish with buttons and beads. Make the petals and poke through the blue hessian.

3. To make the stalk, roll up a rectangle of green fabric and bind with green thread all along its length. Couch this in position by sewing up on one side of the stalk and sewing down on the other.

4. Cut leaves out of thick green fabric. Sew these into position, padding them slightly with toy filler.

5. Slip a cane into the top and hang.

3-Dimensional Sunflowers and Vase

Resources
- Materials used for Group Wall Hanging (page 58)
- Materials used for Papier Mâché Balloon Vases (page 10)
- Stiff wire or thin cane
- Green fabric and thread, needle

Approach

1. To make the sunflower heads, follow steps 1–4 of the Group Wall Hanging.

2. Roll a length of stiff wire or thin cane in green fabric. Bind all along its length with green thread.

3. Cut a circle of green fabric the same size as the back of the sunflower head. Make a snip in the centre of this. Sew the green circle to the back of the sunflower neatly around the edges leaving a small section unsewn. Stuff the back of the flower with toy filler. Sew up the opening.

4. Push the end of the stalk through the hole in the centre of the green circle and either sew or glue with latex adhesive. If the stalk of the flower is made from wire, bend the top slightly. If the head wobbles about too much stick the bottom edge of the flower to the stalk.

5. To make the vase, see Papier Mâché Balloon Vases, page 10.

Flower Cushion

Approach

1. Cut out a circle of material for the centre of the flower. Either stitch this onto the square of hessian or use latex glue.

2. For the petals, cut strips of fabric about 4 centimetres wide and 10 centimetres long. Cut the ends diagonally to form petal shapes.

3. Working from the back, use a sharpened clothes peg to poke the petals through the hessian to the front. Work around the flower centre, making two rows of petals. Cut the leaves in the same way and work one row of leaves.

4. Cut out a square of coloured fabric for the back of the cushion. With the wrong sides of the fabric facing you, sew the front piece to the back of the cushion using back stitch. Leave an opening for stuffing. Turn right sides out, stuff the cushion and sew up the opening.

Flower Hanging

This could be a group or class project.

Approach

1. Let each child work on a 30-centimetre square of hessian to produce a cushion front as above. Use as many colour combinations as possible.

2. Sew the squares of hessian together in strips by overlapping the edges. Sew the strips together.

3. Sew braid over the joins and bind the edges with brightly coloured fabric. Make a slot at the top for a pole for hanging.

Button Mirror Frame

This is a way of giving new life to old vanity mirrors.

Resources
- Old vanity mirror
- Carton card
- Latex glue (optional)
- Double-sided adhesive tape
- Closely woven fabric or hessian
- PVA glue
- Buttons
- Curtain ring

Approach

1. Draw around the mirror on a piece of carton card. Trim the card to the required frame size.

2. Cut a second piece of card the same size. Fix the mirror to the card with glue.

3. Cut out the mirror shape from the first piece of card, making the hole slightly smaller than the mirror.

4. Cut a piece of closely woven fabric slightly larger than the card. Place the card with the hole in it on the fabric and draw around the hole. Remove the card and sew buttons onto the fabric around the mirror shape.

5. When complete, fix the fabric to the card frame with double-sided tape. Cut out the middle section of fabric covering the hole but leave enough fabric to turn to the back. Snip all the way round to ease the fabric. Turn it to the back and glue.

6. Using the PVA glue, attach the frame to the card holding the mirror. Fold the edges of fabric back over both pieces of card and glue at the back. Cut a piece of felt and glue over the raw edges at the back.

7. Sew on a curtain ring for hanging.

Flower Mirror Frame

For Flower Frames use hessian rather than a closely woven fabric. Cut strips of brightly coloured fabric or plastic bag about 6 centimetres wide and 10 centimetres long. Prod these through the hessian following the mirror line. Work three circles of plastic bag or fabric strips. Trim the pegged strips as short as you wish. Complete as above for Button Mirror Frame.

Variation

Instead of working three circles of prodded strips, cover the whole front of the mirror frame with prodded strips of plastic in different colours. Clip very short to give a fluffy pile.

Button Pictures

Resources
- Coloured fabric
- Needles and embroidery thread
- Buttons
- Carton card
- Double-sided adhesive tape
- PVA glue
- Curtain ring

Approach

1. Draw a picture onto a piece of coloured fabric, keeping the design very simple.

2. Sew around the outline of the picture using running stitch, back stitch or chain stitch depending upon the ability of the children.

3. Fill in the design by sewing on buttons. Use a thick embroidery thread as this will hold the buttons securely with fewer stitches.

4. When finished, attach the sewing to a piece of carton card using double-sided adhesive tape. Turn the edges to the back and glue.

5. Cut a piece of felt or other fabric and glue to the back. Sew on a curtain ring as a hanger.

Button Tubs

Resources
- Small lidded containers
- Coloured fabric
- Buttons
- Needle and thread
- Double-sided adhesive tape
- PVA glue

Approach

1. Measure the height and the circumference of the tub. Cut a piece of fabric this size plus a small allowance for overlap.

2. Sew buttons all over the fabric.

3. Glue the fabric to the container with PVA glue or use double-sided adhesive tape.

Beaded Sun-Catchers

These sun-catchers were inspired by the dreamwebs of the native North American peoples. You will need plenty of beads for a whole class project so start collecting broken necklaces well in advance.

Resources
- Wire ring or thick card ring
- Coloured yarns
- Beads

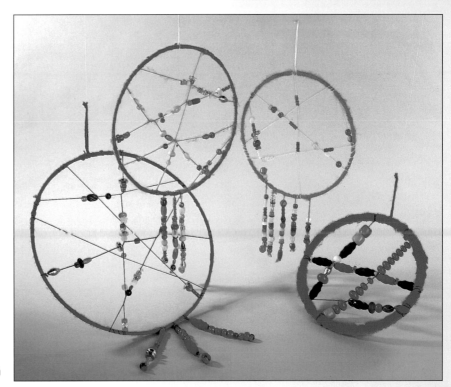

Approach

1. Make a wire ring by bending a length of wire into a circle and securely taping the ends together.

2. Wrap a brightly coloured yarn around the ring. Secure the end.

3. Tie a length of yarn to the ring and thread on some beads. Secure the yarn at the other side of the circle by turning it around the ring several times. Remember to keep the yarn as taut as possible.

4. Thread on some more beads and re-cross the circle. Where two lengths of yarn cross wrap the second around the first to prevent the beads from sliding backwards and forwards across the whole width of the ring. Continue in this way until the space seems evenly divided.

5. Thread short lengths of beads and tie to the bottom of the ring.

Bubble Wrap Sun-Catchers

Resources
- Wire or thick card ring
- Large bubble wrap
- Marker pen

- Necklace beads, buttons, marbles, large sequins, glass nuggets, shiny sweet wrappers

- Coloured yarns
- Clear adhesive tape
- Needle and thread

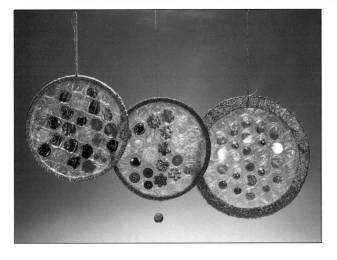

Approach

1. Place the ring onto the bubble wrap and draw around it with a marker pan. Cut out on the inside of the line so that no ink shows.

2. Make a slit in each bubble and insert the button, bead or other shiny object. Work along one row at a time. Seal the slits with clear adhesive tape.

3. Wrap the ring with yarn or thin strips of fabric. Place the bubble wrap into the ring and sew into position with thin thread.

4. Hang beads from the bottom of the ring if desired.

Embossed Foil Plates

Approach

1. Cut slits into the sides of a foil dish or plate at regular intervals and flatten the sides down. Place it on a padded surface, such as a thick magazine or newspaper.

2. Using a blunt pencil draw the design onto the foil dish. Go over the lines several times to make them wider. Try filling in spots to create the impression of studs on the reverse side. Take care not to press too hard or the dish will tear.

3. If desired, the finished plates can be sprayed with gold or bronze paint.

Resources
- Large foil dish or plate
- Magazine or newspaper
- Pencil
- Gold or bronze paint (optional)

Foil Pendants

Resources
- Small foil dishes
- Carton card
- Pencil
- PVA glue
- Gold or silver knitting yarn

Approach

1. Cut slits into the sides of the dish at regular intervals, stopping just short of the base of the dish. Flatten the dish out.

2. Place the flattened dish onto a piece of carton card and use a blunt pencil to outline the base of the dish, pressing down firmly. Emboss the design onto the base.

3. Remove the dish from the card and you should see a clear outline of the bottom of the dish imprinted on the card. Cut out the card around the imprint.

4. Glue the foil (raised side uppermost) to the card shape. Bend the sides of the dish to the back of the pendant and glue. Roll the edges on a hard surface.

5. Pierce a hole through the pendant and thread with gold or silver knitting yarn.

Carnival Shakers

Resources
- Coloured plastic bags
- Foil dishes
- Thin coloured card
- Rice or split peas
- Stick (garden cane or thin dowel)
- Brightly coloured fabric
- Clear adhesive tape
- Mini stapler

Approach

1. Cut narrow strips of plastic bag. Gather into two bunches and secure the ends with tape. Staple these to either side of a foil dish.

2. If desired, cut card shapes and staple these to the rim of the dish or thread wooden beads onto strong yarn and staple these so that they hit the dish when the shaker is twisted.

3. Put a little rice into one of the dishes. Put the other dish on top to form a lid. Staple the rims of the dishes together, leaving a space through which to push a stick.

4. Tape the stick securely to the dishes. Bind the stick with strips of brightly coloured fabric.

Bottle Top Rattles

Resources
- Thin, soft plastic bottles (preferably coloured)
- Metal bottle tops
- Coloured plastic bags
- Needle and strong yarn
- Hammer and nail
- Double-sided adhesive tape

Approach

1. Using a hammer and a nail, make holes in the centres of 20 bottle tops.

2. Thread a long needle with strong yarn. Tie a large knot at the end. Thread on two bottle tops. Stitch through the bottle to the opposite side and thread on two more bottle tops. Sew a large knot in the thread and cut off the end. Repeat this process until all the tops are sewn to the bottle. Dab a spot of PVA glue onto each knot to secure the top.

3. Decorate the top of the bottle by cutting small strips of plastic bag and tying together in the middle to form a flower or bow. Attach this to the top of the rattle with double-sided adhesive tape.

Bottle Top Figures

Resources
- Metal bottle tops
- Plastic bottle tops
- Thin flexible wire
- Hammer and nail
- Wire cutters

Approach

1. Using the hammer and nail, punch a hole in each bottle top. You will need about 70 tops for a figure. It is probably easier to punch a few tops at a time and build the figure up in stages.

2. Punch or drill a hole in the side of a plastic bottle top – this will be used for the head. Thread a length of wire through the hole bringing the two ends together. Twist the wire two or three times and open the two ends of the wire out to form the arms of the figure (see diagram a).

3. Slot another length of wire, twice the length of the intended body and legs, through the loop just under the head. Bring the ends together and twist tightly below the arm wire (diagram b).

4. Thread the bottle tops onto one arm to the required length. Snip the wire and bend the end over into a loop to form a hand and to hold the bottle tops in place. Repeat for the other arm.

5. Thread the remaining two wires together through the bottle tops to form the body (diagram c). When this is long enough, twist and separate the wires to form the legs. Thread tops onto each leg wire and bend the ends up into loops to form feet and to hold the bottle tops in place (diagram d).

6. The figures could be suspended on nylon line or set into tubs of plaster.

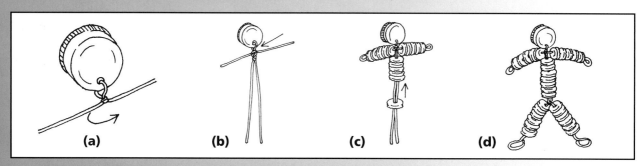

(a)   (b)   (c)   (d)

Wire and Wool Figures

Resources
- Flexible wire
- Wire cutters
- Oddments of wool
- Tin lids
- Sawdust
- Double-sided adhesive tape
- PVA glue

Approach

1. Cut a length of wire long enough to form the arms and head. Bend the wire to form the head. Twist the wire to form the neck and open out to make the arms. Bend the ends up into loops for the hands.

2. Make the body and legs as for Bottle Top Figures, page 66.

3. Wind wool around the wire figure, building up layers until the figure is sufficiently large. Sew in the ends of wool with a needle or simply glue them down. Put a strip of double-sided adhesive tape around the head before winding with wool. Add hair and facial features.

4. The figures can be mounted on tin lids using a mixture of sawdust and thick PVA glue. Paint when dry.

Bits and Bobs People

Resources
- Plastic and metal bottle tops of all shapes and sizes, corks, pen tops, film canisters, beads, buttons, the plastic casings from old felt-tipped pens, ring pulls from cans, small objects that can be threaded on wire
- Pipe-cleaners
- Flexible wire
- Wire cutters
- Hammer and nail
- Plaster and tin lids or thin thread

Approach

1. Hammer a hole in each bottle top. Hammer two holes if it is going to be used as a hat.

2. Cut a length of wire long enough to form the body and the legs when folded in half.

3. Fold the wire in half. Thread the ends of the wires through the holes in the bottle-top hat. Twist the two ends of wire together and thread on a bead or cork for a head. Add something small for a neck.

4. Cut a length of wire or pipe-cleaner for the arms. Felt-tipped pen casings can be cut to size and threaded onto wire for arms and legs. Thread the wire or pipe-cleaner through the two body wires and twist it around them to form the arms.

5. Punch holes in the rim of a lid for a body or thread on buttons or a cork. Larger bottle tops can be used as skirts. Ring pulls can be added as feet.

Wire Jewellery

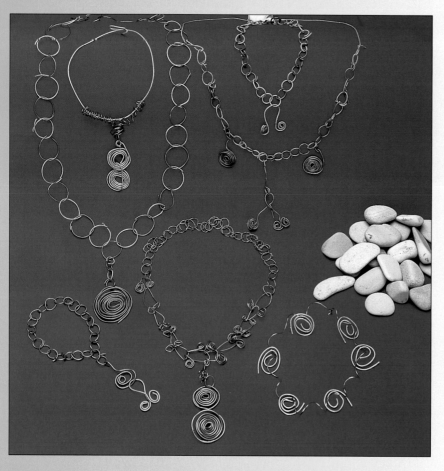

Resources
- Flexible wire (stripped electrical flex, oddments of garden wire or plastic-coated wire)
- Wire cutters
- Mini, long-nosed pliers

Let the children have a period of experimentation to get used to the tools and the wire.

To Make a Coil or Spring

Wind a length of wire around a pencil or length of dowel. Remove the coil and either squeeze the links closer together or leave them open. Snip the coils of the spring to make jump rings. Make plenty of jump rings. When joining them squeeze together well.

To Make a Flat Spiral

Grip the end of the wire with the long-nosed pliers and wind the wire part way round the tip of the pliers. Remove the pliers. Grip the coil flat between the pliers and keep turning it, gradually winding on more wire. Once a coil has been started it can be turned in the fingers. Several coils can be joined together with jump rings to form a necklace.

To Make a Shaped Spring

Make a spiral at each end of a piece of wire. Coil them up until they meet. Bring the spirals together by closing like a book. Using long-nosed pliers, pull the ends of the wire out to open up each spiral. These long spirals can now be hung from a chain.

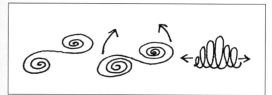

To Make a Chain

Bend a length of wire into a U-shape. Make a tiny flat spiral at each end of the wire. Squeeze the U-shape together just above the spirals. Make several of these. To make a chain, hold one link by the spirals, slip the bend of another link into this and pull up. Bend the spirals of the second link upwards and flatten.

Variation

Introduce stones, sticks and shells into the jewellery making. Coil stones or sticks with copper wire. Look for shells with holes that can be threaded onto wire or linked with jump rings. (See also Acknowledgements, page 2.)

Ballerinas

These little figures might develop from a study of movement and dance. Reference could also be made to the work of Degas.

Approach

1. Cut three 30-centimetre lengths of wire. Make a loop in the centre of one length by coiling the wire around a small pot or thick dowel to form a head. Twist the wire together two or three times to form a neck and then open the wire out to form arms. Bend the ends up into loops (see diagram a).

2. Cut a coloured plastic bag into strips about 6 centimetres wide and 15 centimetres long. Gather the strips up and hold in the centre with a second length of wire. This wire will make the legs (see diagram b). Use the last length of wire to bind the plastic strips and leg wire together. Bend the plastic strips and leg wire downwards. Bind round the fold with clear tape to hold in position. Bend the ends of the leg wires up into loops to form feet.

3. Pass the end of the body wire through the head until the desired body length is reached, then bend the wire over and twist around the body (diagram c). Clip off any excess wire. At this stage the head and arms will flop around a little but will become firm when wound with wool.

4. Bind a little double-sided adhesive tape around the hips and head of the figure before winding with wool. Trim the skirt and bend the arms and legs into position. Set the dancer into a small lid filled with plaster.

Resources
- Wire
- Coloured plastic bags
- Clear adhesive tape
- Wool
- Lid
- Plaster

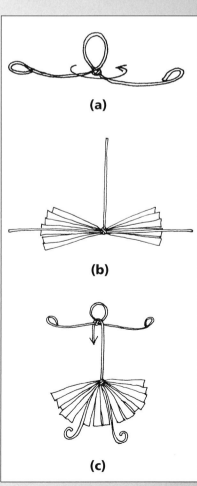

(a)

(b)

(c)

Outdoor Nightlight Holders

Recycle old tin cans into decorative lanterns.

Resources
- Shallow tin cans
- Wire
- Glass beads
- Hammer and nail

Approach

Make sure that the tops of the cans have been removed smoothly and there are no sharp edges.

1. Punch three evenly spaced holes near the rim of the can with a hammer and nail.

2. Cut three lengths of wire and thread them into the holes, twisting the ends down into the inside of the can.

3. Thread each length of wire with beads, leaving enough wire at the top to bend the ends over into a loop.

4. Decorate the can with sequins, shiny items or fabric.

5. Put small nightlights or candles in the cans.

⚠ **Never leave children unsupervised with burning candles.**

Wrapped Tin Cans

Resources
- Tins
- Oddments of wool, felt or fabric
- Double-sided adhesive tape
- PVA glue

Approach

1. Put several strips of double-sided adhesive tape down the sides of the can (three or four if using a large can, two for a small one).

2. Decide upon a scene and start wrapping wool from the bottom of the can upwards.

3. When the can is covered, cut out felt motifs and glue in position.

4. Cut out a circle of fabric and glue onto the lid.

Beaded Plaques

These attractive plaques are made from broken or discarded jewellery.

Resources
- Tin lids
- Beads
- String or wire
- Hammer and nail
- PVA glue

Approach

1. Using a hammer and nail punch a hole at the top of a tin lid and thread with string or wire to form a hanger.

2. Spread thick PVA glue into the lid. To make the shields, start in the centre with an earring or pendant. Then add circles of beads around this until the lid is full.

3. To make the number plaques, place a circle of beads around the outside edge of the lid. Make the number shape and fill in all the spaces.

4. Leave the plaques for several days to dry thoroughly.

Broken Crockery Mosaics

These mosaic plaques would be fun to make as part of a Greek or Roman topic.

Resources
- Broken crockery
- Hammer
- Polythene bag
- PVA glue or plaster of Paris
- Tin lids
- Protective goggles

Approach

1. Make a collection of chipped or broken crockery and old plates.

2. Break these into mosaic-sized pieces by placing them a few at a time in a strong polythene bag and tapping sharply with a hammer. Ensure the bag is tied securely to prevent flying chips. Wear protective goggles and wear gloves when handling the broken crockery.

3. Make a hanger as above and spread plaster of Paris or PVA glue on the tin lid. Arrange the broken pieces of crockery to suit. Small rigid containers such as plant pots can also be covered.

Textile Flowers – A Group Wall Hanging (page 58)